Today's Struggles, Tomorrow's Revolutions

Today's Struggles, Tomorrow's Revolutions

Afro-Caribbean Liberatory Thought

Drucilla Cornell

ROWMAN & LITTLEFIELD
Lanham • Boulder • New York • London

Published by Rowman & Littlefield
An imprint of The Rowman & Littlefield Publishing Group, Inc.
4501 Forbes Boulevard, Suite 200, Lanham, Maryland 20706
www.rowman.com

86-90 Paul Street, London EC2A 4NE

Copyright © 2023 by The Rowman & Littlefield Publishing Group, Inc.
All rights reserved. No part of this book may be reproduced in any form or by any electronic or mechanical means, including information storage and retrieval systems, without written permission from the publisher, except by a reviewer who may quote passages in a review.

British Library Cataloguing in Publication Information Available

Library of Congress Cataloging-in-Publication Data Available
ISBN 978-1-5381-6848-6 (cloth); ISBN 978-1-5381-6849-3 (paperback); ISBN 978-1-5381-6850-9 (ebook)

To my comrades and friends Roger Berkowitz, Jane Anna Gordon, Lewis R. Gordon, Paget Henry, and Peter Hudis: I have never thought of writing as a lonely or isolated activity. I have always thought with and through my comrades and friends. This has never been more the case than this book, and it is dedicated to them.

Contents

Acknowledgments	ix
Revolution Today: Struggles That Shake Our World	xiii
Chapter 1: Struggle in Motion: Rethinking Violence	1
Chapter 2: The Struggle in Process: On Revolution and Black Liberation	25
Chapter 3: The Spirit of Struggle: On Dialectical Materialism and Political Spirituality	47
Chapter 4: Future Struggles: Stardust People and Democratic Socialism	81
Conclusion: Tomorrow's Revolution: A Call to Action in Salvador Allende's Last Words	105
Notes	109
Index	121
About the Author	131

Acknowledgments

I want to start with thanks to Roger Berkowitz. Roger gave me a critique of my first attempt to discuss Hannah Arendt's engagement with Frantz Fanon and especially as she reads what she understands to be his position on violence. His thoughtful and insightful remarks led me to go back to Arendt and rewrite that entire section. As the director of the Hannah Arendt Institute at Bard, he has played a key role in bringing the significance of Hannah Arendt for contemporary politics. Roger and I go way back. As a graduate student after reading my book *The Philosophy of the Limit*, he met me at a conference and asked if he could take a year off from his graduate program to study Hegel with me. At that time, Hegel was at the heart of my own philosophical journey and very controversial in Anglo-Analytic philosophy. I said yes. We plowed through Hegel's *Science of Logic* in German. Roger was then and is now an infinitely better Germanist than I was or am. For the next fifteen years, we met every week and worked our way through the classics of German Idealism. We were on page 673 of *The Critique of Pure Reason* when Roger's wife, Jenny Lyn Bader, a rightfully well-known playwright, went into labor and Roger became a father. But our collaboration did not stop, even though we never came back to page 673. At this time, we initiated a book series called *Just Ideas* with the late Helen Tartar at Fordham Press. We also collaborated on an article on Clint Eastwood's *Mystic River*, which became part of my book on Eastwood as a director.

And now we come to Jane Anna Gordon. *Just Ideas* proudly published Jane Anna Gordon's *Creolizing Rousseau* and Michael Monahan's *Creolizing the Subject*. These two books introduced creolizing as a new way of doing revolutionary and decolonizing political theory. Jane was one of the founders as well as the former president of the Caribbean Philosophical Association. Both her work and her leadership led me to ask her if she would be interested in co-editing a book that would creolize the great revolutionary Marxist theorist Rosa Luxemburg. She jumped in. I could never have done it without her. In the middle of the pandemic, we organized a class with Michael Lardner of the Marxist Education Project with the authors in our book on the 150th anniversary of Rosa's assassination. In a grim time, working together to celebrate Rosa was one of the things that kept me going. Jane is now one of the editors of the series in which this is being published. I am honored that this book is included in this series. I thank her for her support and critical insight.

There are almost no words to express the central role Lewis Gordon has played in my life as a critic and a supporter, including becoming a regular of the uBuntu Project I founded in South Africa. I could not have built the project without his wisdom and advice. I first became familiar with Lewis's work when our beloved editor Maureen MacGrogan asked to review one of his early books. I was blown away. Since then, I have devoured his work. He has influenced my thinking in more ways than I can express. He is unquestionably one of the great philosophers of the twentieth and twenty-first centuries. I turn to him constantly as I shift my own thinking away from Eurocentrism and he is always there. This book had to be rewritten to integrate his latest new book *Fear of Black Consciousness* because the power of his argument had to be reflected in my own book. Lewis was also one of the founders of the Caribbean Philosophical Association, which has enabled new revolutionary decolonizing ways of thinking, including my own. His generosity and enabling of others including my own work is exemplary. Without his friendship I would be a different person. Most recently his characteristic generosity led him to volunteer to do the index of this book.

Paget Henry, like Lewis Gordon, is one of the leading philosophers of our time. He is also an important sociologist and historian particularly of the revolutionary movements in the Caribbean. In the last fifteen years he has become one of my most important critics. I turn to him again and again. His distinction between the vertical and horizontal aspects of revolution shaped the entire organization of this book. I rewrote chapter 3 because of his critical comments and his rightful insistence that I needed to grapple seriously with C. L. R. James's comrades like Tim Hector who never gave up on James's program of a radical democratic socialist society in the Caribbean. I am grateful for his attention to my work. His brilliance and insight have informed so much of what I have written in many years. I am blessed to have such an interlocutor.

Peter Hudis is unquestionably one of the leading Rosa Luxemburg scholars in the world. As one of the leaders of the Rosa translation group, her collected works will finally be available in English. I turned to him again and again when Jane and I were editing our book, and I've done so here as well. Indeed, I bombarded him with questions which he always patiently answered. Peter was also the secretary to Raya Dunayevskaya. She and C. L. R. James formed the Johnson-Forest Tendency in 1945. It is no exaggeration to write that Peter knows C. L. R. James's revolutionary activism and theory inside out. I am so grateful for the time and attention he gave this book.

I owe more than I can say to Madeleine Disner, my assistant. She is a brilliant theorist in her own right and a careful and thoughtful editor. She read this entire manuscript out loud with me, a grueling job indeed. I am in her debt for her commitment and care.

Stephen Seeley worked with me on chapter 1, which will be published as a shorter article. We have worked together for many years. I am grateful for his collaboration.

I also want to thank my friends at the Waverly Diner. As soon as outdoor dining became a possibility, the Waverly provided a community outlet, including a place to meet and write. Without them I would not have completed this manuscript. They showed the very best of the exhausting job of being essential workers in a difficult time.

My daughter is the light of my life. She has designed all the covers of my books after 2000. I thank her for spending her enormous talent on my projects. But more importantly I am just thankful for her.

I am so appreciative of all support I have been given by the comrades to whom I dedicate this book. I began a long journey in 2001 when after my trip to South Africa I founded the uBuntu Project. Like many others I had become critical of Eurocentrism. But I knew that I needed to educate myself in African Philosophy. I was the student not the teacher, even though I was ultimately awarded a National Research Foundation Chair in *Indigenous Ideals, the Living Customary Law and the Dignity Jurisprudence of the South African Constitutional Court* when I was a faculty member at the University of Cape Town. When the Caribbean Philosophical Association was founded, I became a committed member. I am still on that journey to re-educate myself, and this book is part of that journey. My comrades were with me every step of the way. Of course, all the mistakes are my own.

Introduction

Revolution Today
Struggles That Shake Our World

People make revolutions. They always have. They always will. Struggles break out and spread like wildfire. Certainly that was the case with Black Lives Matter. No one can predict the shape of the future because mass movements themselves create new conditions and new ways of being together that force us to rethink the very concepts of revolution. That said, however, it is certainly possible to critique when transformative revolutionary movements have failed in their promises to realize the great ideals that were the basis for their organizational struggles. A classic example is the African National Congress (ANC), unquestionably a revolutionary movement in the old-fashioned sense of an armed struggle that sought nothing less than the seizure of state power and the radical transformation of both government and social life. In his foundational book *Inequality in South Africa*,[1] economist Solomon Terreblanche argues that the transition and the transformation of South Africa has been partial. Yes, Black people could finally become citizens of their own country, could vote, could assemble, and could own property. But the reason he insists that the transition was *partial* is that the more left-wing Reconstruction and Development Programme (RDP) were not adopted by the ANC even though it seemed, for at least a while, to be the direction of the economic transformation of the post-apartheid country. Yet, during Mandela's own time as president, the ANC made it clear that there was no meaningful alternative to neoliberal capitalism and that such alternatives were non-negotiable. The political transformation was therefore partial because there was no *economic* transformation and, as a result, the majority

Black population actually lived in even greater poverty than it did under apartheid. In his follow-up book, *Lost in Transformation*,[2] Terreblanche argues that because of the failure to adopt a radical economic transformative program, the revolutionary struggle of the ANC had failed. Political power meant nothing if it was not matched with politics being taken into the economic realm and, with it, the democratization of means of production.

The Freedom Charter of the ANC was explicitly socialist, including the nationalization of all the main resources of South Africa. For Terreblanche, however, the failure of economic transformation meant that there was no real meaningful revolutionary change in South Africa despite the great achievement of Black people becoming citizens of their own country. Of course, Terreblanche in no way means to denigrate that achievement. But what I want to emphasize in this book is the importance of political economy and economic change, without in any way saying economic change is separable from revolutionary *political* transformation. Indeed, as the reader will see in the discussion of Lenin and Luxemburg, nationalization of means of production is not the same as the radical democratization of the economy that someone like C. L. R. James will later say is at the very heart of what socialism would demand. Socialism, for me, will always have at its heart economic transformation, but it must transform all social relationships at all levels of society. No one underscored that point more powerfully than Rosa Luxemburg. It is not a choice between economic transformation and a radical change in who we are as human beings. The philosopher Paget Henry emphasizes both by distinguishing between what he calls "horizontal revolution," which involves sweeping economic transformation, and "vertical revolution," which takes us into the realm of radical change in who we are as human beings.[3] I will discuss this distinction throughout this book. The two must come together in what Frantz Fanon reminds us would be a new species of the human.[4]

I cannot know what a revolution will look like, but I want to point to ways forward that at first might not even seem revolutionary at all. The campaigns of Bernie Sanders for president in 2016 and 2020 advocated forms of social democracy that were controversial particularly in US electoral politics. Of course, the Democratic Party mobilized all of its forces against the Sanders campaign to make sure he was never selected as the presidential nominee. There is no question that the Democratic

Party is a party of the capitalist ruling class, but out of the Sanders campaign an organization called Our Revolution was formed. Of course, the reader's and indeed my own first response might be to roll our eyes and say, "What is revolutionary about this? Is this not just a lukewarm form of social democracy?" I want to suggest that the insistence that the United States needs a revolution is itself significant, and Sanders's program is within the US a major challenge to values of neoliberal capitalism and is incompatible with it. Simply put, the program of Our Revolution and the demands of the Sanders campaign were not seen as compatible with the continuation of capitalism as it has been left in its unregulated chaos in the US, with inequalities that are unimaginable. Is Our Revolution a revolutionary organization? Could it be? Is Black Lives Matter revolutionary in its demand that we need to abolish prisons and rethink police security? I do not know what the revolutionary impact of these organizations will be. What I can suggest is that the only way to "know" is to get involved and participate, and then together we will see exactly what turn these organizations might take.

The Sanders campaign labeled itself progressive. Now, there are other institutions in the Democratic Party like Elizabeth Warren's progressive democrats that also use the word "progressive." But the word implies *progress* and, for me, "Progress toward what?" is the fundamental question. At least in Sanders's program, which he has enumerated on a number of occasions, progress is toward a transformation of the economic structure of advanced neoliberal capitalism. Donald Trump calls everyone a socialist, but the truth is that only Bernie Sanders ever identified himself as a Socialist—indeed, initially running for mayor of Vermont as a Socialist. The word "progressive" then obscures what we are supposedly progressing toward. Warren has said she is pro-capitalism; Sanders has never backed down from identification as a socialist. I am not romanticizing the Sanders campaign. I simply want to point out that a campaign that started as nothing in 2016 picked up incredible momentum precisely because it pointed toward a socialist future. A future that the campaign itself could barely articulate and yet in that bare articulation it mobilized millions of young people to find hope. Obama called his book *The Audacity of Hope*, but he failed to tell us what we were hoping for, and his presidency showed us how powerless the Democratic Party is in its ability to do even the most moderate reforms. This powerlessness is even more evident in Biden's failure to pass his Build Back Better bill. The point here is that we don't know, and cannot know, when these kinds of movements can become *revolutionary*. Even if the old notion of revolution as the armed struggle to seize state power may no longer be possible, I believe revolutionary change in the direction toward socialism is indeed possible, and nobody can tell us it is theoretically impossible. That is the philosophical point: there is a limit to what theoretical reason can predict.[5]

BLACK REVOLUTION AND REVOLUTIONARY POSSIBILITY

Black Lives Matter is not just about George Floyd or the innumerable murders of Black men and women at the hands of the police. Of course, it *was* about those men and women who were cruelly killed as if their lives did not matter at all or were buried under the fantasies of the terrifying Black monster. But the movement's demands went to the *reorganization of the state* with such programs as defunding the police and the abolition of prisons. But were these demands explicitly against *racial capitalism*? Often they were. Were they for socialism? Often they were. Indeed, the concept of "racialized capitalism" moved into trade publishing because of Black Lives Matter. Think for example of the *New York Times* best seller, *How to Be an Antiracist*. The author, Ibram X. Kendi, explicitly talks about racism and the need to struggle against racialized capitalism. The popularization of racialized capitalism as a target of struggle grew out of the struggles in the streets. The other point I have emphasized is that these programs develop *in the streets*—they do not arise out of the heads of intellectuals. If we intellectuals have a job at all, it is to read what those demands signify. The struggle against racialized capitalism demands complete transformation of the economy and an end to neoliberal capitalism.

In his powerful book *Fear of Black Consciousness*,[6] Lewis Gordon writes that George Floyd's poignant cry, "I can't breathe," is not just the desperate plea of one man with a police knee on his neck. It is part of the reality of anti-Black racism where opportunities are choked off by police brutality, yes, but far beyond police and the system of incarceration, which is part of how Black people are contained, are the voices that are stifled by the endless struggle of so many Black people to just survive another day. As he explains, no one is born with Black Consciousness, it grows out of facing oppression just because of how one is seen to be in a racist society. For Gordon, when Black consciousness becomes a cry for freedom, it is not only political but revolutionary. Is the struggle against dehumanization just for Black people? Not at all. It is a struggle against disempowerment that blocks us all in our efforts to breathe freely and to live in a world worthy of justice. The Caribbean thinkers, including Gordon, that I focus on in this book, remind us again and again of both the possibility and the necessity of revolution as integral to Black liberation. As we will see in chapter 2, which focuses on the writings of C. L. R. James, Black liberation is universal in scope.

TONI MORRISON ON FASCISM

To hold onto the promise of revolution is in no way to deny that we live in ominous times where fascism is a real threat. In her now almost prophetic article "Fascism and Racism," Morrison writes,

> Let us be reminded that before there is a final solution, there must be a first solution, a second one, even a third. The move toward a final solution is not a jump. It takes one step, then another, then another. Something, perhaps, like this:
>
> 1. Construct an internal enemy, as both focus and diversion.
>
> 2. Isolate and demonize that enemy by unleashing and protecting the utterance of overt and coded name-calling and verbal abuse. Employ ad hominem attacks as legitimate charges against that enemy.
>
> 3. Enlist and create sources and distributors of information who are willing to reinforce the demonizing process because it is profitable, because it grants power, and because it works.[7]

Morrison's first three steps are blood chilling because it describes so much of our current political reality. For the reader's information, I list the rest of the steps that Morrison suggests in the footnotes.[8] Step nine speaks directly to how mindlessness and apathy are rewarded with trivial entertainment's pseudo-successes, such as hits on the internet.

Morrison makes it clear that fascism is not right populism at all because it feeds on its purges of any real democratic action. It is capitalism with a naked face, with no more pretense that there is something like a public good. It needs racism because there has to be an enemy. But the enemy is exploited through marketing. Again, to quote Morrison,

> Fascism talks ideology, but it is really just marketing—marketing for power.
>
> It is recognizable by its need to purge, by the strategies it uses to purge, and by its terror of truly democratic agendas. It is recognizable by its determination to convert all public services to private entrepreneurship, all nonprofit organizations to profit-making ones—so that the narrow but protective chasm between governance and business disappears. It changes citizens into taxpayers—so individuals become angry at even the notion of the public good. It changes neighbors into consumers—so the measure of our value as humans is not our humanity or our compassion or our generosity but what we own. It changes parenting into panicking—so that we vote against the interests of our own children; against **their** health care, **their** education, **their** safety from weapons. And in effecting these changes it produces the perfect capitalist, one who is willing to kill a human being for a product (a pair of sneakers, a jacket, a car) or kill generations for control of products (oil, drugs, fruit, gold).
>
> When our fears have all been serialized, our creativity censured, our ideas "marketplaced," our rights sold, our intelligence sloganized, our strength downsized, our privacy auctions; when the theatricality, the entertainment value, the marketing of life is complete, we will find ourselves living not in a nation but in a consortium of industries, and wholly unintelligible to ourselves except for what we see as through a screen darkly.[9]

If fascism is not right populism, it is also not authoritarianism. The only authority is marketability. There is no authority worthy of respect. Certainly not government of the public good or the great ideals of dignity, freedom, and equality. Of course, fascism needs a brutal repressive apparatus to purge those who are the enemies of anything-goes marketability. The repression is against the racialized demons. January 6 was an expression of white male desperation of nostalgia for a racist world. Those white males should have "more"—the more of unionized jobs. In rage they tried to show a masculinity that has been undercut by a neoliberal economy that outsources the jobs of the unionized white working class. Those rioters could only see through a screen darkly.

ON WHITENESS

Here I come to one of my key points: there is no such thing as *white* with a capital *W*. I disagree, then, with Ibram X. Kendi when he writes white with a capital W, although he is careful to distinguish *racist power* from *white people*: "To be antiracist is to never mistake the global march of White racism for the global march of White people. To be antiracist is to never mistake the antiracist hate of White racism for the racist hate of White people."[10] There is no such being as a "White person" because *white* always carries within it a class dimension as well as ethnic divisions. The class/race divide misses the class-ridden nature of *racialized capitalism* embroiled in the fantasy of Whiteness. It has nothing to do with skin pigmentation, by which I do not mean that anyone can be whatever color they choose (far from it). I have distinguished between *position, identity*, and *identification*.[11] I am *positioned* as white. There is a material reality to white skin privilege and I do not feel "fragile" in recognizing white skin privilege. Nor do I feel "guilty." Under racialized capitalism, race pervades all identities. The next step after recognizing the materiality of white skin privilege is to join the struggle against racialized capitalism. To be antiracist is to *disidentify* with supremacy and therefore with White as an identity with its brutal history of racism. This call to disidentification takes us one step beyond Kendi. But this disidentification is not simply a negative: "I am not that." It is also a call to join collective action.

In my own case, it led me to join the Civil Rights Movement. I grew up in a completely segregated world. Most people who grew up around me had no real encounters with African Americans, let with alone Latin Americans or Asian Americans. I lived in a white community where being a Democrat and being a Communist were the same thing. But the difference in my life was that I regularly traveled to Watts, an African American community, with my grandmother. For complicated reasons, my grandmother was involved in Orisha Spirituality, a practice that originated in Africa and came to the Caribbean and the United States with the slave trade. My grandmother was the first woman to become an owner of a printing company in Los Angeles. She remained the only female owner for fifty years. She did not have colleagues, she had competitors. It was a lonely road, so she sought out a Vodun priestess in Watts to consult with her dead husband about the endless complexities of running a printing company. Questions about firings, about purchasing technology, and other business decisions. I am often asked if I believe in spirit possession or the ancestors, but it is not a matter of belief. What I do know is that some people are empowered to open doors to the beyond and let the dead speak. But I do not tell this story to focus on Orisha Spirituality, as important as it is in our world today. Rather, I tell this story because this was my first regular contact with Black people. We took the bus into Watts. I never saw another white person there. I suppose some were surprised to see white people, but if so they were too polite to show it. Once, because of a change of bus schedule, we got a bit lost on the way to the priestess. My grandmother approached a middle-aged Black man doing yard work and asked for help. He kindly took us to her house. All those years we were treated with respect. We were never robbed or attacked in any way. As the years passed, people smiled and waved. We were a woman in her late fifties and her granddaughter, pretty easy targets, but I was not afraid. There was no reason to be.

Years later, I confronted the violence of whites against desegregation. *Brown vs. Board of Education*[12] constitutionally rejected the so-called separate but equal doctrine of Jim Crow, but white schools were not complying with the law, and the violence against Black children was photographed for all to see. The National Guard had to be called in to protect the small number of Black children in Little Rock, Arkansas. I kept contrasting the way in which my grandmother and I had been treated to the way these white mobs were fueled by hatred into violence. One school did comply with the desegregation law, but to my horror, one morning, a bus of eleven Black eight-year-olds was set on fire by a crowd of white adults. I kept imagining the horror of children being burned alive, begging for help. Two days later, I volunteered to attend an all-Black high school. I was fifteen and my parents blocked my effort. I then became involved in the movement to register African Americans to vote. I am often asked if I was motivated by guilt or shame. I was motivated by horror. Horror is not a feeling in an individual subject. It is material as it seeps into the world around us, materializing in violence that turns contact into blood and guts. To fight white supremacy is to fight against that horror that has bled into all of our lives. To undo that horror is to open the spaces to breathe so we can reach out to one another. That is what Gordon emphasizes.

I am talking about my own experience in my decision to attend an all-Black high school, but I want to make it clear that there's a difference between being against segregation and being for busing. I now want to turn to another story, a story where a young man rebelled against busing, and show how that rebellion itself does not necessarily mean support for segregation, let alone anti-Black racism. I turn to Michael MacDonald's book *All Souls*,[13] a memoir of growing up in the predominantly Irish American and desperately poor Southie community in Boston. Southie became the very symbol of poor whites being the engine of white supremacy in their militant rejection of busing. But here we see how the designation of who is "really" White and the function of racist forces can define the story. After all, the Irish have a rocky history of making it as "really" White.[14] The "really" White, elite public schools were not included in the busing program. Wealthy suburban white schools, which were 100 percent white, were untouched by busing because the criteria of "racially imbalanced" meant schools that were over 50 percent Black, not 100 percent white.[15] The busing program was to bus white students from Southie to Roxbury, an overwhelmingly Black community, and vice versa. Both communities had schools that were underfunded—a true understatement. Southie had the highest number of teenagers on welfare in the city. South Boston High had the highest dropout rate in Boston. So, what was the point of this busing program? To provide the kids with a better education? Obviously not. MacDonald himself dropped out of school and went on to get his GED. As MacDonald writes in his article on Southie's battle against busing, the only real beneficiary of this battle was Whitey Bulger, the crime boss that ran Southie for many years. Unemployed and with no possibility of a decent education, white youths were easy recruits for Bulger's many criminal activities. The busing program was set up to fail.

Desperately poor whites can be infected by racism, but they are not its cause. Kendi does write about racialized capitalism as at the root of the problem, but he does not spend enough time explaining *why*, as I hope to do in this book. MacDonald's story shows disidentification as he moves into community activism and works closely with community organizations. MacDonald lost several siblings to Bulger's criminal control over Southie, but as he goes into the church to light candles, he does not do so just for the siblings he tragically lost but for all souls. Hence the title of his book: *the struggle against racialized capitalism is for all souls*. And that is the meaning of the disidentification with Whiteness by white people. *All Souls* beautifully tells of one man's journey to that conclusion.

This is not a book directed against white people. But it is a call for us to carefully examine and come to terms with the way in which racial demonization undermines the crucial effort to constantly reinvent and rebuild our humanity together.

Chapter 1

Struggle in Motion
Rethinking Violence

. . . eight minutes, forty-six seconds . . .
This is how long a Minneapolis police officer knelt on the neck of a Black man, George Floyd, as he complained that he could not breathe, begged for his life, and called out for his mother until his body eventually went still—yet another of the nearly 1,300 Black lives snuffed out by law enforcement in the United States since the shooting of Michael Brown in 2014.[1] Within hours, as a chilling video of the incident made its way across the internet, demonstrations began in Minneapolis, and within days, and in spite of the ongoing coronavirus pandemic, more than twenty million people in more than four thousand cities in every part of US territory, from Utah to Charlotte Amalie, and throughout the world, from Buenos Aires to Tehran to Tokyo, had taken part in a new wave of Black Lives Matter protests.[2, 3] Across the streets and screens on which the recent uprisings are playing out, one of the most widely circulated slogans has been the well-known quote attributed to Angela Davis that says, "In a racist society, it is not enough to be non-racist. We must be *anti*-racist." The current popularity of this quote makes sense, as the fact that more people than ever before are participating in these demonstrations indicates people's increasing awareness that they must actually *do* something to combat racism. And yet, it has been striking how often this quote has appeared alongside variations of the sentiment that the protests are righteous so long as they remain "non-violent," so long as protestors do not use physical force or destroy property. But is there not a dissonance between these two positions? Can one, truly, be *anti*-racist while insisting that all anti-racist action must remain

1

non-violent? If racism is, in theory and in practice, a form of violence—as the video of George Floyd's lynching, among so many others, makes spectacularly evident—then would we not have to read the subtext of Davis's statement as "In a racist (=*violent*) society, it is not enough to be non-racist (=*non-violent*). We must be anti-racist (=*anti-violent*)"? And, in that case, as Davis insists that we do with "non-racist" and "anti-racist," we would have to think very seriously about the difference between *non*-violence and *anti*-violence. Presumably the latter involves a more active stance than the former: to be non-*x* is merely to say that *a* is not *x*, while to be *anti*-x is to say that *a* is *opposed* to *x*. So, as Davis says, any person can define herself as "non-racist" without doing anything to *oppose* racism. But what would this mean in the case of violence? We might identify ourselves as "non-violent," but what are we actually *doing* to *oppose* violence?

This raises questions about the use of physical force against persons or property as a form of *anti*-violence: might such actions be tactics for *opposing the violence* that defines everyday life in conditions of colonial-racial capitalism? Of course, such questions are bound to make liberals uncomfortable, for the commitment to "non-violence" is one of the most unshakeable pillars of liberalism. But one need not look too deeply to see that, in a profound sense, violence constitutes the repressed heart of liberal conceptions of politics. Since Hobbes's *Leviathan* (1651), the state has been understood as the contractual displacement of a violent "war of all against all" to the authority of the sovereign, which maintains what Max Weber called a "monopoly" on the legitimate use of violence.[4] The sovereign state is then justified in deploying this transferred violence only in the protection of its citizens—or, more precisely following John Locke, the protection of their *property* (including their personhood conceived as property)[5]—from threats, foreign and domestic. Theoretically, the social contract demands that *all* citizens, equally, relinquish the use of violence to the sovereign state; however, in a state in which property is the basis of racial and class supremacy, or what legal theorist Brenna Bhandar has appositely termed "racial regimes of ownership," this leads to a two-tiered system of those who have property (and personhood) worth defending, and those who do not.[6] Thus, violence is fundamentally aligned with property: those with property have access to the only legitimate form of violence—the entire machinery of the state—while those without property are merely subjected to the state's authority without any recourse to (legitimate) violence of their own. This means that no matter how brutal the forms of violence deployed by state apparatuses in enforcing racial and class supremacy, the dispossessed are never justified in deploying violence themselves, even in self-defense.[7] It is thus no surprise that the first targets of movements against white supremacy and colonization are typically the police and military forces. And, from this philosophical position, we can see why liberals, throughout history, have tended to remain very ambivalent toward armed struggles. Why their commitments to "social justice" and a fundamental "right to protest" end when property is threatened. Why the equivalence is frequently made between Black life and white property—"It is horrible that the police killed another Black person, but this destruction of property has to stop." Why there is a liberal fetishization of "non-violent" figures like Gandhi and Martin Luther King Jr., or why figures like Nelson Mandela and Angela Davis can only be celebrated insofar as their involvement in armed movements can be minimized or erased.

In this chapter, I want to challenge the incoherence of this position—and particularly its central assumption that we can grapple, politically, with something like "violence" as opposed to "non-violence." What this metaphysical dichotomy does is create a moral distinction between Good ("non-violent") and Bad ("violent") political movements, where especially since the so-called War on Terror the "Bad" is associated with "terrorism."[8] No doubt, the question of violence is probably the most difficult question that any political theory can confront—indeed, Étienne Balibar has called it the very limit of (European) political philosophy.[9] But as history and present events attest, the question is as inescapable as it is difficult. And unfortunately, it is here—where the stakes could not be higher—that Euro-American political theory is often at its most uninspired. My point in this chapter is not to "defend" violence. It should go without saying that no political thinker in the United States should dare to write a critical word about violence without starting from a recognition of the horrific atrocities perpetrated by the US government at home and throughout the world—especially the brutal and systematic suppression of revolutionary movements that has done more than anything else at keeping the world's socialist experiments from ever getting off the ground. But that is not my central point. After all, to paraphrase Foucault, it is not for thinkers to say whether or not violence is necessary, justified, or legitimate. It is enough that people do undertake violence in the name of revolution that makes it a question we must confront.[10] And for this purpose, I argue that we need a new conceptual vocabulary, which I will introduce here—one that dispenses with the limited and untenable division between "violence" and "non-violence" in favor of a spectrum of *revolutionary action*.

THINKING ABOUT VIOLENCE: ARENDT AND FANON

Within the canon of Euro-American political theory, few thinkers have taken the question of violence more seriously than Hannah Arendt, herself a refugee from Nazi Germany. For this reason, her work makes a good starting point for my purposes here. In her famous essay "On Violence" (1969), Arendt laments the lack of sophistication afforded to the subject of violence and attempts to analytically disentangle what she sees as a number of conflated terms. She therefore proceeds to make a set of important distinctions that separate *violence* from related concepts such as *power*, *authority*, *force*, and *strength*. The most important of these, from Arendt's own perspective, is the distinction between power and violence. "Power," according to Arendt, "corresponds to the human ability not just to act but to *act in concert*," while violence is "distinguished by its *instrumental* character."[11] We can more fully understand the distinction that Arendt is making here, as well as her clear preference for "power" over "violence," by reading it through the foundational distinctions she makes in *The Human Condition* (1958) between labor, work, and action. To summarize it very simply: *labor* refers to the most basic activities of producing and reproducing life, *work* is instrumental activity that produces a material object, and *action* is activity through which humans realize ourselves as such in the public sphere.[12] Thus, while the species-level activities of labor involve human beings only as living organisms (*animal laborans*), we become human (*homo faber*) through work that intervenes in the natural order so as to make a distinctly *human* mark on it. But it is only through *action* that we reach the realm of *freedom* in which we can fully actualize our humanity: that is, only by action that transcends the natural cycles of labor and the instrumental rationality of work—both being constrained by forms of *necessity*—can we be truly free and truly human. This is why, for Arendt, action is inherently political and politics is the epitome of action. From this point of view, then, violence is always bound to instrumental necessity, thoroughly determined by its means and ends, which categorically prevents it from rising to the heights of properly human action, to politics, and to the realm of freedom. While violence might be an effective *means* of accomplishing a certain end, and while that end might sometimes justify the means, only the collective exercise of *power*—the very essence of political action—can constitute something that is an *end in itself*. Indeed, given her idealistic conception of politics, Arendt actually *opposes* power and violence: "Politically speaking," she writes, "it is insufficient to say that power and violence are not the same. Power and violence are opposites: where the one rules absolutely, the other is absent. Violence appears where power is in jeopardy, but left to its own course it ends in power's disappearance."[13] Thus, for Arendt, there is nothing more *powerful* than *collective political action*.

As appealing as this theoretical schema might be, its practical limitations become clear when we look more closely at the larger context of her essay: what might be called a screed against the participants—especially the students (and particularly Black students)—in the global uprisings of 1968 who, in Arendt's estimation, were driven by violence instead of properly political action. A principal target of her ire in this respect is the students' embrace of the writings of Frantz Fanon, most notably his own essay "On Violence," the infamous opening chapter of *The Wretched of the Earth* (1961). As far as Arendt is concerned, Fanon is one of the "preachers of violence" who promotes and glorifies precisely the kind of violent activity that she considers to be a political dead end.[14] Instead, she implores her readers to draw on the republican tradition as the proper bearer of the legacy of revolutionary thought and practice.[15] But it is the nature of Arendt's criticism of Fanon that makes it particularly illuminating for rethinking the question of violence and revolution in this chapter. In the first instance, it is important to note the way in which Arendt treats *The Wretched of the Earth* as just another volume of abstract political theory rather than as a dispatch from the frontlines of the final year of the Algerian War—the horrifically violent culmination of a century of brutal colonial rule—no matter how much Arendt would like to praise the "restraint" of the French.[16] Of course, I need to emphasize that Arendt is often not dealing so much with Fanon himself as with Sartre's reading of Fanon. Even so I must underscore this point: Fanon's text is not a "theory of violence"; it is a desperate attempt to make sense of the first decade of African decolonization in the hopes that it might help guide the rising tide of liberation movements sweeping through the colonized world. Erasing this context, it is unfair to pit Fanon's writings as some sort of antithesis to the European republican tradition, ignoring, of course, that the underside of the tiny handful of "republican" states—if indeed they can even be called that—is the brutal colonization of more than 90 percent of the planet.

But more to the point, unlike Arendt, I read *The Wretched of the Earth* as profoundly *anti-violence*: against the torture and maiming, against the massacres and murders, against the rapes and violations, against the poverty and hunger, against the humiliation and dehumanization, against the psychic degradation and cultural destruction to which the Euro-American imperial powers have subjected the vast majority of the planet's population for centuries. Indeed, the main type of violence described on the pages of that book are the forms of "extreme violence" that Étienne Balibar has named "cruelty." Cruelty, for Balibar, has two modalities: on the one hand, an "ultra-subjective" violence by which individuals and groups incessantly create various Others and target them with hatred, abuse, and death; and, on the other hand, an "ultra-objective" violence by which "impersonal" systems and processes produce a whole population of "disposable human beings"—that is, *the wretched of the Earth*.[17] These forms of violence take place beyond any rigid distinctions between the social, political, economic, and natural: in the *favelas*, slums, shantytowns, and refugee camps, where the planet's surplus are abandoned to pandemics and ecological catastrophes, to genocides and ethnic cleansings, to gangs and traffickers; the zones of "slow violence," where the afterlives of war, colonization, toxic dumping, and resource extraction are billions of systematically disabled, debilitated, and worn out bodies, populations, and infrastructures that can barely sustain life. And, most cruelly of all, where future generations are incapacitated before they are even born, destroying even the possibility of resistance.[18] The "common denominator" of these forms of cruelty, as Balibar has put it, "is that they reduce human beings to the condition of things, beginning by suppressing their individuality and treating them as quantities of residual 'pieces.'"[19] It is *this* violence—which Fanon will describe as *atmospheric*—that *The Wretched of the Earth* is most concerned with.[20]

If anyone, it is Sartre (most famously in his preface to *The Wretched of the Earth*), and not Fanon, who romanticizes the violent "outbursts" of the colonized. Indeed, it is explicitly at Sartre that Arendt aims her most overt criticism of the anti-colonial movements:

> In no case, as far as I know, was the force of these "volcanic" outbursts, in Sartre's words, "equal to that of the pressure put on them." To identify the national liberation movements with such outbursts is to prophesy their doom—quite apart from the fact that the unlikely victory would not result in changing the world (or the system), but only its personnel. To think, finally, that there is such a thing as a "Unity of the Third World," to which one could address the new slogan in the era of decolonization "Natives of all underdeveloped countries unite!" (Sartre) is to repeat Marx's worst illusions on a greatly enlarged scale and with considerably less justification. The Third World is not a reality but an ideology.[21]

Fanon, however, even in defending the necessity of the armed struggle against colonization, in no way romanticizes violence. In *The Wretched of the Earth*, he offers a sophisticated analysis of both the "grandeur" *and* the dangers of spontaneity. And as a practicing analyst of patients on both sides of the Algerian War, he is all too aware of the devastatingly traumatic effects of an armed struggle and consistently worries, throughout *The Wretched of the Earth*, that the toll a struggle for decolonization takes on its leaders might make them incapable of leading the difficult process of postcolonial reconstruction. To quote Lewis Gordon's very different take on Fanon's attitude toward violence: "The system produces monsters, but Fanon's sobriety emerges from his admitting and demonstrating that even its overcoming is monstrous."[22]

But does Arendt think that insurrections against such monstrous cruelty are never inevitable or necessary? After all, this would surely be an indefensible position for the author of *The Origins of Totalitarianism*. In fact, such struggles do seem to register when, in the closing paragraph of "On Violence," Arendt argues that "disempowerment" is an "open invitation" to the eruption of violent revolt:

> Again, we do not know where these developments will lead us, but we know, or should know, that every decrease in power is an open invitation to violence—if only because those who hold power and feel it slipping

from their hands, be they the government or be they the governed, have always found it difficult to resist the temptation to substitute violence for it.[23]

Although I profoundly disagree with this shallow description of the horror of being denied every meaningful kind of action under colonialism as an existential as well as political robbery of one's human being,[24] as well as the flat equivalence she draws between the "government" and the "governed" (an equation that, once again, precisely elides the *damned*), it is nevertheless a mistake to read Arendt as idealizing non-violence or condemning violence as "evil."[25] I will return shortly to how an analysis of colonialism can never rest on Arendt's notion of government as "institutionalized power," and thus any analysis of decolonial anti-violence can never be captured by her critique of violence, but the nuance that I hope to bring in my own critique of non-violence is poorly served by turning Arendt into a simplistic theorist of "non-violence." Her analysis is rich enough to distinguish between different forms of violence depending on the type and degree of power behind it.[26] Indeed, she also recognizes that "under certain circumstances violence—acting without argument or speech and without counting the consequences—is the only way to set the scales of justice right again" (although I would certainly take issue with her clarification that "Billy Budd, striking dead the man who bore false witness against him, is the classical example").[27] And she even argues that to deny these actions for justice would be dehumanizing. Still, such acts, by her definitions, are always *apolitical* and cannot lead to new forms of power, let alone the creation of a new humanity demanded by the struggle for decolonization. "Violence," she writes, "can destroy power; it is utterly incapable of creating it."[28]

This brings us to the limits of a Eurocentric analysis of violence such as Arendt's in which action and instrumentality, power and violence, can be separated, even theoretically. Without an analysis that *centers* the conditions of colonialism and racism, we can thus never develop the sort of nuanced rethinking of violence, non-violence, and anti-violence that we so desperately need in our time. As Fanon tells us, colonization can be understood as nothing other than an institutionalized form of instrumental activity by which colonizers "*fabricated* and *continue to fabricate* the colonized subject" in the interest of wealth accumulation.[29] In reality, then, the colonial-racial capitalist state is not the institutionalization of the collective *power* of the people, but a *violent* ad hoc conglomerate of military and militarized police forces, parastatal mercenaries, mafias, cartels, and corporations working to protect the interests of the tiny ruling class. Judged by Arendt's own standards, then, any administration rooted in colonial domination, white supremacy, and capitalist exploitation is not a "government" at all, but a totalitarian *state of terror*. And as Aimé Césaire captures it in his *Discourse on Colonialism* (1955), such a state eliminates all possibilities of *human* inter-*action* as *everyone* is sucked into a perpetual cycle of violence and instrumentality in which certain human beings are merely the means by which others pursue their aims:

> Between colonizer and colonized there is room only for forced labor, intimidation, pressure, the police, taxation, theft, rape, compulsory crops, contempt, mistrust, arrogance, self-complacency, swinishness, brainless elites, degraded masses. No human contact, but relations of domination and submission which turn the colonizing man into a classroom monitor, an army sergeant, a prison guard, a slave driver, and the *indigène* into an instrument of production. My turn to state an equation: colonization = thingification.[30]

As objects, instruments, and tools, the wretched of the Earth are not even living beings (*animal laborans*), for even the most basic activities of "life" are simply a means of (re)producing the system of wealth and domination, thus collapsing any distinction between *labor* and *work*. In this way, what Fanon calls "decolonial *counterviolence*" is the very opposite of an instrumental assertion of revenge against the backdrop of a non-violent government: it is the assertion of *collective action* by which the damned transcend the state of terror that holds them in an *enforced* cycle of instrumentality at the deepest levels and finally become *human*. "Decolonization," as Fanon famously puts it, "is truly the creation of new human beings. But such a creation cannot be attributed to a supernatural power: The colonized 'thing' becomes a human through the very process of liberation."[31]

So perhaps if Arendt read Fanon differently, we could see that for both of them political action is at least crucial to what it means to be human. Arendt insists,

> What makes man a *political* being, is his *faculty for action*; it enables him to get together with his peers, to act in concert, and to reach out for goals

and enterprises that would never enter his mind, let alone the desires of his heart, had he not been given this gift—to *embark on something new*. Philosophically speaking, to act is the *human* answer to the condition of natality. Since we all come into the world by virtue of birth, as newcomers and beginnings, we are able to start something new; without the fact of birth we would not even know what novelty is, all "action" would be either mere *behavior* or *preservation*.[32]

But are collective association, getting together with peers, acting in concert, speaking in public (let alone in one's native language), and all the other modes of "world disclosure" that Arendt associates with action not *exactly* what have been systematically and cruelly stripped from the wretched of the Earth? What if the simple fact of your birth as Black in a white supremacist world means you are lucky if even "preservation" is allowed, let alone "novelty"? And is not the very imagination of something other—something *new*—the ultimate target of the violence of colonial-racial capitalism so that the cycle of cruelty might perpetuate itself as if it were merely natural? As Angela Davis poignantly points out:

> One of the major examples of the violence of racism consists of the rearing of generations of Black people who have not learned how to imagine the future—who are not now in possession of the education and the imagination that allows them to envision the future. This is violence that leads to other forms of violence—violence against children; violence against partners; violence against friends.[33]

And is this not to damn them to a fate of inhuman cruelty where every desire of a different future, let alone the means of achieving it, is extinguished before it is even born?

Thus, I do not find in Fanon any "praise of violence."[34] I see, instead, only a profound horror at the cruelty that the Euro-American imperial powers have inflicted upon untold billions of human beings, a profound rage at having been dispossessed of all other forms of action to make life meaningful, and a profound hope that taking on the immense burden of decolonial counterviolence might, perhaps, engender a new beginning for *all* of humanity. This, of course, is where Arendt's critique of violence is most opposed to Fanon, since, for her, any violence—even decolonial counterviolence—is instrumental and *cannot* create new forms of power and a new humanity. But it is probably the difference in the *spirit* of Fanon's and Arendt's writings that makes the most difference here in formulating a theory of revolutionary violence appropriate to the struggles of our time. "Dreams," as Arendt writes, "never come true."[35] Appearing on the streets of New York in 2021, however, is graffiti that reads "Dream until you *fight* to make it your reality." I would add that the notion of "political spirituality" I have developed elsewhere accepts with humility that we can never *know* in advance what we can do together, which leaves space for the big dreams that calls us to action. I think Fanon accepted this as well. Yes, he saw clearly the toll that the armed struggle for liberation, socialism, and decolonization could take on those who gave everything for freedom, and yet there was hope. A worried, hesitant hope, certainly, but what hope is not? As the people erupting in anti-violent insurrection against the nightmare of racist cruelty in our streets today understand clearly, struggle is the only way forward and, thus, we must both dream *and* fight for that which may only be a hazy vision now.

TOWARD A NEW VOCABULARY OF VIOLENCE

One of the merits of Arendt's analysis is that, by taking the question of violence and revolution seriously, she formulates a critique of violence with recourse to *political* rather than moral or religious principles. From this point of view, in which violence is understood at the level of instrumental activity, violence is merely one way of accomplishing political goals. And locked into the cycle of means and ends, in which the end is often lost in the means, such activity can, at best, achieve its stated *end* but it can never constitute a new *beginning*. Thus, as far as politics goes, there are more effective—more *powerful*—modes of action available. But, as with most liberal political theory, this analysis has to bracket the atmospheric violence—the cruelty—of colonial-racial capitalism so that power struggles (i.e., political action) can take place in a theoretical vacuum of "non-violence." This is precisely what Angela Davis was getting at when, in a 1972 interview from a California state prison during her incarceration under false charges of murder, she pointed out exactly why asking the question of whether revolutionary violence is "appropriate" without beginning *from* the violent context of everyday life for Black people in the US makes no sense:

When you talk about a revolution, most people think "violence," without realizing that the real content of any kind of revolutionary thrust lies in the principles and in the goals that you are striving for, not in the way you reach them. On the other hand, because of the way this society is organized, because of the violence that exists on the surface everywhere, you have to expect that there are going to be such explosions, you have to expect things like that as reactions. If you are a Black person and live in the Black community all your life and walk out on the street every day and see white police surrounding you . . . when you live under a situation like that constantly . . . and then you ask *me* whether *I* "approve" of violence? I mean that just doesn't make any sense at all. Whether *I* "approve" of guns? I grew up in Birmingham Alabama. Some very, very good friends of mine were killed by bombs—bombs that were planted by racists. I remember, from the time I was very small, I remember the sounds of bombs exploding across the street, our house shaking. I remember our father having to have guns at his disposal at all times because of the fact that at any moment we might expect to be attacked. The man who, at that time, was in complete control of the city government—his name was Bull Connor—would often get on the radio and make statements like, "N****** have moved into a white neighborhood, we better expect some bloodshed tonight." And sure enough: there would be bloodshed. After the four young girls, who lived very close—one of them lived next door, I was very good friends with a sister of another of them, my sister was very good friends with all of them, my mother taught one of them in her class. In fact, when the bombing occurred, one of the mothers of one of the young girls called my mother and said "Can you take me down to the church to pick up Carol? We've heard about the bombing and I don't have my car." And they went down and what did they find? They found limbs and heads strewn all over the place. And then after that in my neighborhood, all of the men organized themselves into an armed patrol. They had to take their guns and patrol our community every night because they did not want that to happen again. I mean, that's why when someone asks me about violence, I just find it incredible. Because what it means is that the person who is asking that question has absolutely no idea what Black people have gone through, what Black people have experienced in this country since the time the first Black person was kidnapped from the shores of Africa.[36]

Here, we see that the problem of instrumentality—violence as a means for political purposes—is, in fact, a secondary problem. And, after all, as Fanon trenchantly notes, nothing has been more effective at instilling in oppressed people that violence is their only route of action—that violence is the only *language* of "world disclosure" that can make a difference—than the all-pervasiveness of violence in colonial-racial capitalism itself:

> In fact, the colonist has always shown them [the colonized] the path they should follow to liberation. The argument chosen by the colonized was conveyed to them by the colonist, and by an ironic twist of fate, it is now the colonized who state that it is the *colonizer* who only understands the language of force. The colonial regime owes its legitimacy to force and at no time does it ever endeavor to cover up the nature of things. . . . The colonist's logic is unrelenting and one is only baffled by the counterlogic of the colonized's behavior if one has remained out of touch with the colonist's way of thinking.[37]

That the dualist ontology of violence/non-violence must first theoretically bracket the violence that constitutes the general atmosphere of colonial-racial capitalism means not only that it is bound to misunderstand why the damned would undertake revolutionary violence, but it also flattens out all violent activity. Of course, one would like to imagine that Arendt would be more sympathetic to the Black Panthers' *end*—a defense of their Second Amendment right to protect their communities from police brutality—than to the Trump militia's libertarian opposition to the COVID-19 lockdown measures. But that the means are the "same" would, for Arendt, perfectly demonstrate the inherent limitations of violence as a form of power or more precisely one that can generate new forms of power activity. On the contrary, I would argue that the difference in these two cases is much more than a question of instrumental ends. Indeed, that I would place the Black Panthers on the side of revolutionary action and the Trump supporters on the side of terrorism is not merely because I "like" Black Panthers and "hate" MAGA extremists, nor even because I support anti-racism and reject libertarianism as a matter of political preference. Rather, there is a deep and profound philosophical difference at stake here that gets to the very heart of what revolutionary thinking must confront with respect to violence.

To fully explain this, I must introduce a new vocabulary of violence and revolutionary action—one that takes off not from a flat ontology of violence versus non-violence but from Fanon's multidimensional distinction between the *atmosphere of violence* and *violence in motion*. Based on this distinction, I will introduce four "levels" of revolutionary activity: *spontaneous insurrectional activity, non-retaliatory anti-violence, self-defense*, and *offensive armed struggle*. These levels differ in the degree to which they incorporate the atmosphere of violence into organized revolutionary activity, but I do not mean to imply that one necessarily leads to another in any linear way. Nor do the levels exist in isolation, as revolutionary movements typically involve all of them in different times and places. But all of them are forms of what Étienne Balibar calls *anti-violence*, which is a *condition of revolutionary action*. Balibar carefully distinguishes anti-violence from both "non-violence" and "counter-violence": while non-violence is merely an abstraction, counter-violence responds to violence with similar violence as a sort of negation of a negation.[38] For Balibar, much of what is called revolutionary violence is actually "counter-violence," which aims to invert the violence of the repressive state apparatuses and, indeed, to "monopolize" it in the form of a new state. This is why the aftermath of revolutionary counter-violence is often a reign of terror, as the new state deploys the very cruelty of what has been overthrown in maintaining its often-fragile hegemony. Arguably, this type of counter-violence is what Arendt has in mind in her critique of violence, but that she does not seem to imagine the possibility of *anti-violence* points to the limits of her ontology of violence/non-violence. And besides, the entirety of *The Wretched of the Earth* could be read as a warning about the dangers of precisely this kind of counter-violence (notwithstanding Fanon's use of the phrase "decolonial counterviolence"). Anti-violence, on the contrary, is what Balibar calls a *"facing up" to violence*:[39] it occurs where the passage from one form of violence to another is *interrupted* by collective action, which Balibar understands as *"insurrection."*[40] As I will argue, following Fanon, any *anti-violent* action necessarily involves setting the atmosphere of violence into motion without which there would be no opportunity for insurrectional rupture. This does not mean, however, that the setting of violence into motion must take the form of *counter*-violence (although we should expect that this will occur). Rather than counter-violence that meets violence with violence in kind, revolutionary action should be understood as a politics of *anti-violence* that sets the atmosphere of violence into motion in order to counter conditions of cruelty with what Balibar calls *"civility."*[41] It is on this basis, then, that I will distinguish our categories of revolutionary action from *terrorism*, which works not to terminate, but to *perpetuate*, the general atmosphere of violence and cruelty. The movement of transformation where the atmosphere of violence is set into motion is what I call *spontaneous insurrectional activity*. This is, in effect, ground zero of revolution—the zero-point of organized revolutionary activity—where the cycle of cruelty is *faced* by collective anti-violent action. As Fanon describes it, this is when the wretched of the Earth begin to channel the violence imposed upon them into the momentum of decolonization:

> But let us return to this atmospheric violence, this violence rippling under the skin. We have seen as it develops how a number of driving mechanisms pick it up and convey it to an outlet. In spite of the metamorphosis imposed on it by the colonial regime in tribal or regional conflicts, violence continues to progress, the colonized subject identifies his enemy, puts a name to all of his misfortunes, and casts all exacerbated hatred and rage in this new direction. But how do we get from the *atmosphere of violence* to *setting violence in motion*?[42]

As I write this, literally thousands of cities in the US and around the world have seen massive uprisings against the cruelty of police brutality and white supremacy. What has happened is that the atmosphere of violence has grown too dense—literally suffocating Black people—and one event, one more lynching of a Black person by the police, causes it to erupt as people set this violence into motion toward a transformative political program. Through this spontaneous insurrectional activity, people not only rupture the cycle of cruelty, name their enemy and find an outlet for their rage. More importantly, they find the first form of public *collective action* capable of giving a sense of direction to the senseless cruelty that is often borne silently, privately, and individually as part of the natural cycle of life in colonial-racial capitalism. Through this collective anti-violent action, they exercise a *civility* that establishes a political community and begin to articulate specific demands for justice, equality, and liberty. Thus, spontaneous insurrectional activity—even when it fails to have the leadership that Fanon reminds us is crucial to any form of organized struggle—is never simply instrumental. Yes, sometimes this form of activity involves counter-violent conflicts with police, instigators, and attacks on private property. (Although let me be clear that the attacks on property are often on enclaves of hideous and obscene white wealth, such as designer boutiques in Soho.) But, for political thinkers, it makes less sense to try to draw a *cordon sanitaire* around these instances than it does to grasp the process of insurrectional activity as a whole: the point is not to isolate the bad "violent" protestors from the good "non-violent" ones, but to see how effective the collective action is at setting the stifling atmospheric violence into motion. As I will discuss at length in the next chapter, the problem with spontaneous insurrectional activity is not that it is merely instrumental and cannot bring about a new beginning, but how to channel the continuity of the ongoing revolutionary struggle from insurrection to insurrection.

Once the atmosphere of violence has been set into motion through collective action, we reach the first level of organized revolutionary anti-violence. This is what I call *non-retaliatory anti-violence*. This type of action goes beyond spontaneous insurrectional activity in that it is constituted by an ongoing, organized, collective channeling of the atmosphere of violence toward a new beginning, but it incorporates into its action the minimum possible degree of counter-violence. But this minimization should not be conflated with "non-violence" in order to juxtapose this level of revolutionary action with the others. The US Civil Rights Movement, for instance, is often held up by white liberals as the exemplary "non-violent" political movement. But when young students sat at lunch counters knowing they would be pulled off of their stools, kicked, and stomped by white adults, was this *non*-violence? When demonstrators marched against the disenfranchisement of Black voters knowing they would be gassed and clubbed by police, was this *non*-violence? When the Freedom Riders boarded buses in protest against the unconstitutional segregation of public transport knowing they would be beaten with pipes, bats, and chains by mixed mobs of Klansmen and law enforcement officers, was this *non*-violence? Some were killed, hundreds if not thousands were brutally injured and never recovered. Was this, in any meaningful sense, non-violent? Outside of the theoretical vacuum of political theory, not at all. Yes, there was often a decision taken not to *retaliate* against their attackers with physical force. For some, like the early Martin Luther King Jr., this was an ethical commitment, while for others it was a *strategic* decision made with the full awareness that any Black person who fought back against a white person would end up lynched, their home burned down, their family and comrades tortured. In fact, many participants in the Civil Rights Movement undertook tactical workshops that specifically trained them how to endure a mob attack without fighting back and, by the end of his own life, Dr. King himself had begun to express serious reservations about the sustainability of a policy of "non-violence" within the horrific cruelty of everyday life of the US.[43] Perhaps it was Malcolm X who captured it best when he suggested that the effect, if not the purpose, of King's "non-violent marching" was to "dramatize the brutality and the evil of the white man against defenseless Blacks."[44] From this perspective, the very efficacy of so-called non-violent action was directly proportional to the amount of cruelty Black bodies could sustain. I would therefore argue that not only is the reliance on the Civil Rights Movement as the basis of a philosophy of "non-violence" historically inaccurate, but it fails to take account of the context of cruelty within which the movement took place. Certainly, the Civil Rights Movement exemplifies an ethical desire to keep counter-violence to a minimum, but even more, it speaks to the practical reality of *non-retaliation* as the safest way of keeping a revolutionary struggle alive in a situation that simply would not allow Black people to counter violence with violence.

This brings us to the second level of organized revolutionary anti-violence: *self-defense*. By "self-defense," in part, I mean the defense of your person: when someone attacks you, you attack back; if someone pulls a gun on you, you pull one on them. But more importantly, "self-defense" in the context of revolutionary action far exceeds the defense of individual bodies and seeks to protect the *collective institutions* established in revolutionary struggles. Oppressed groups often, by necessity, set up their own institutions for providing childcare, education, healthcare, food, and, yes, their own defense forces. And what are such endeavors—which aim precisely at the collective creation of a counterpublic set of institutions—if not an attempt to move beyond the labor of everyday life to *political action*? Take, for instance, the Black Panther Party, who were often labeled as "terrorists" in contradistinction to the "non-violent" organizations of the Civil Rights Movement. The Panthers' call for armed self-defense was never merely a reaction to the US state apparatuses undertaking murderous violence against Black revolutionaries and their communities, but part of their larger "Ten-Point Program," which called for "land, bread, housing, education, clothing, justice, and peace."[45] As co-founder Huey P. Newton described the Black Panthers' expansive conception of "self-defense":

> When we used "for Self-Defense" we realized that all oppressed people or legitimate revolutionary oppressed people never are the aggressors; *all of their action is in self-defense*. The Vietnamese people are merely using self-defense; it's the capitalistic, imperialistic exploiters who initiate violence and aggression. So whatever the people do for their liberation, for their freedom, is a self-defense tactic. We've expressed time and time again, that when we used the words "Self-Defense," it also meant defending ourselves against poor medical care, against unemployment, against poor housing and all the other things that poor and oppressed people of the world suffer.[46]

This is why one of the Black Panthers' most important programs was their famous "Free Breakfast for Children Program," which defended thousands of Black children every day in Oakland, California, and beyond from the cruelty of starvation and malnutrition. Similarly, the Revolutionary Afghan Women's Association (RAWA)—also labeled as "terrorists" by many in the US—have established much-needed institutions like schools, hospitals, gynecological clinics, literacy and vocational courses, and self-defense training in rural Afghanistan and have fought to defend these institutionalized attempts at giving women and children a chance at life from attacks by the Taliban and the ravages of four decades of war.[47] What we see in these cases is that defensive operations are never merely *re*-active counter-violence, but a necessary part of the *active* and *anti-violent* struggle to build—literally with blood, sweat, and tears—a new collective order out of a state of cruelty that aims at systematically destroying anything and everything they might do to make their lives worth living.

When revolutionary action goes beyond a defense of lives and institutions, it enters what I would call the *offensive armed struggle*. This type of action aims at the total channeling of the atmosphere of violence into motion in the form of an offensive movement against the racial-colonial capitalist state. "The existence of an armed struggle," as Fanon puts it, "is indicative that the people are determined to put their faith only in violent methods. The very same people who had it constantly drummed into them that the only language they understood was that of force now decide to express themselves with force."[48] We see this, for instance, when the African National Congress established its armed wing, uMkhonto we Sizwe (MK; Spear of the Nation). In apartheid South Africa, Black people were literally not citizens in their own country—they could not vote, own property, write, protest, or participate in anything like a democratic public sphere. In fact, if two or more Black people met publicly, it was considered an "insurgency." And when they did try to protest peacefully against the so-called pass laws in Sharpeville in 1960, it ended in a massacre by the police forces. MK thus began, in part, as a defense force to protect the Black population. But it was also engaged in an offensive struggle to overthrow the horrific state of terror that was the apartheid "government" and establish a democratic South Africa. No movement enters offensive struggle glibly, as Fanon makes clear, and certainly not for the thrill of destruction or "praise of violence" that Arendt seems to think. But I would emphasize even more than Fanon that an armed struggle is not ultimately defined by "counter-violence" in Balibar's sense that fights cruelty with cruelty. In South Africa, the armed struggle was actually limited by an official Code of Conduct drafted by former Constitutional Court Justice Albie Sachs. This code placed ethical and legal limitations against specific forms of extreme violence and cruelty, demonstrating that far from the armed struggle being the *most* violent and cruel, it is the form of revolutionary action in which the violence and cruelty must be controlled by anti-violent *civility* to the highest degree.[49] Indeed, such a Code of Conduct was designed precisely to prevent what Arendt feared as the inherent tendency arising from the instrumentality of violence: that any means can become justified in the name of the end. What the ANC recognized is that once violence has been set in motion in the name of justice and freedom, every step must be taken to prevent the struggle from sliding back into the atmosphere of violence, from falling back into the forms of cruelty that the struggle is confronting. This is not to deny that there is an element of "instrumentality" in an armed struggle—after all, its tactics are a means of seizing state power or establishing some form of political hegemony. But much more than this, through the *complete* setting of violence into motion, the armed struggle seeks to permanently transform the atmosphere of instrumental violence and cruelty institutionalized by the colonial-racial capitalist state into a *government*, in Arendt's sense, that is rooted in the *collective power of the people*. In a word: *revolution*.

By replacing the ontological dualism of violence/non-violence with this spectrum of revolutionary action—different degrees of organization in setting the atmosphere of violence in motion toward a new humanity—we are no longer bound to distort or erase history in order to fetishize good "non-violent" movements while demonizing other movements as "terrorism." We no longer have to ignore or bracket the institutionalization of instrumentality and cruelty that constitutes "the state" in colonial-racial capitalism. We no longer have to argue against the only forms of collective human action available to the wretched of the Earth. We no longer have to consider the Black Panthers and armed Trump supporters the same, even "philosophically speaking." Indeed, we can now coherently distinguish revolutionary action from terrorism without drawing the line on the basis of whether or not we "approve" or "disapprove" of a movement's political "ends," or on a moral metaphysics of good and evil. Terrorism is not part of the setting of violence into motion toward transformation—it is not anti-violent action aiming to counter cruelty with civility—it belongs to the very *atmosphere of violence*. Sometimes, as in the case of a Palestinian suicide bomber, this takes the form of a desperate counter-violence, when an individual or group attempts to bring some of the cruelty under which they have been forced to live into the lives of those who impose it—or those who would look the other way. Fanon writes of the tragedy of this type of terrorism, which seeks, through one spectacular demonstration, to invert the atmosphere of violence onto the oppressive regime but for this same reason cannot set this violence in motion toward a new beginning. Much worse, however, is the case of white supremacist terrorists who use fear, terror, and brutality to keep other people "in their place." This is the kind of "extreme violence," or cruelty, that Balibar calls "ultra-subjective" and here the terrorists are effectively acting as vigilante agents of the racial-colonial regime, whose own institutionalized violence they feel has not been effective enough in maintaining white supremacy. In both cases, terrorist violence is *purely instrumental*, purely a means to an end. And by failing to challenge the idea that human lives are of no real value, terrorism is ultimately a form of nihilistic cruelty that has nothing to do with the forms of anti-violent revolutionary action that aim to set violence in motion in the struggle for a new humanity.

REVOLUTIONARY ANTI-VIOLENCE: AN ETHICAL IDEAL AND A POLITICAL STRUGGLE

It is precisely the instrumentality of the violence deployed by repressive state apparatuses that allow us to differentiate it from the anti-violence of revolutionary action. I mentioned Justice Albie Sachs above, but let us briefly return to his history as a comrade in struggle to liberate South Africa from the horrific state terrorism that was apartheid. As Sachs explains, Oliver Tambo, a leader of the ANC in exile, had heard disturbing rumors that some members of the armed struggle had moved from revolutionary anti-violence into forms of terrorism that the ANC completely rejected no matter how desperate the situation. Tambo's response was that even the armed struggle needed to be guided by ethical principles—and I would add here that these principles were particularly associated with the indigenous ethics of *uBuntu*, which understands that human beings are tied together in an affective web of relations in which any action against another person radiates into *all* forms of individual and collective activity.[50] Tambo's concerns were passed onto Sachs, who was asked to help develop the Code of Conduct precisely so that the means deployed in struggle could *never* be separated from the ideals for which they were fighting. To quote Sachs:

> I was then asked at an ANC conference in a small Zambian town, called Kabwe, to introduce the Code of Conduct. It operated at three levels. At the lowest level, it dealt with the legal processes to be followed in the case of people who came drunk to branch meetings and who were just disruptive, and so on. You dealt with that *politically*. The next level related to people who stabbed, stole, assaulted, crashed motorcars, and drove while drunk. We developed regional tribunals with a limited range of penalties to handle these alleged offenders. At the highest level, the Code of Conduct dealt with grave offences aimed at destroying the organization. These included killing members, assassinating leaders, using bombs and poison to cause mayhem. In dealing with these issues, very special procedures were laid down. Offences were defined with some precision. Evidence had to be led, and could be challenged. Defenders were provided. A range of permissible punishments was provided. There was a system of appeal. I think it is the most important legal work I've ever done.[51]

Why is this so important here? The idealization of "non-violence" and the contrast between "good" and "bad" political movements at least implicitly assumes that all political violence is shaped entirely by instrumental rationality rather than ethical ideals. But did the South African Defence Forces ever write a code of conduct to limit the extent of their massive campaign to kill off the struggle against the cruelty in which Black South Africans had lived their lives for four centuries? Of course not. I refer to the ANC's Code of Conduct here because it shows us that even in an offensive armed struggle, revolutionary action is not defined instrumentally by its *ends*, but by the *ideals* that animate the struggle. I need to emphasize this point: *ends are not the same as ideals* and it is the latter that are at stake in revolutionary action. The instrumental use of cruelty and terror by police forces as nothing other than the means of maintaining colonial-racial capitalism is therefore of a completely different order than revolutionary action which aims to turn an atmosphere of violence into a struggle that is bound not by any *end* but by the *never-ending* ideals of freedom, equality, and justice—ideals that demand a collective praxis of being human. Thus, even if the armed struggle sets the greatest degree of the atmosphere of violence into motion, this does not—at least not necessarily—entail the abdication of ethical ideals of *anti-violence*. And in this, it can be completely distinguished from the violence of the state and from terrorism—which, I must admit, cannot be so clearly delineated from one another. What armed struggle cannot be so easily distinguished from, however, are the other forms of anti-violent action to which it is often unfavorably counterpoised: non-retaliation and self-defense. I am well aware that some so-called national liberation struggles have undertaken forms of guerilla warfare that have involved murder, torture, rape, genocide, and the kidnapping of children as slaves and soldiers. But any movement that thinks that such forms of terror and brutality are justified in the name of the struggle has completely lost sight, in the dense thicket of instrumentality and cruelty, of the ethical—and, indeed, the *political*—ideals of the project they are supposedly undertaking: the creation of a new humanity. Putting aside for a moment that such forms of extreme violence are often tied to assertions of phallic authority—a point I will take up later in this book—from the perspective of our vocabulary of violence, terrorism always misses the anti-violence that is the ethical and political heart of revolutionary action. Simply put: raping someone or cutting someone's head off has nothing to do with revolution, *period*. But, on the other hand, white liberals who stand up and decry the destruction of property, armed self-defense, or even armed struggles to seize the state, in the name of "non-violence" fail to understand how these struggles are the only way to move forward toward a new beginning. While the distinction between "violence" and "non-violence" might be possible *in theory*, it is *never a political reality*. Indeed, as I have shown through my critique of Arendt, such a position fundamentally misunderstands the violence and cruelty that constitute the very atmosphere of everyday life for billions of people in conditions of colonial-racial capitalism. And yet, by reading Arendt "against" herself, her work provides the elements for a new theory of citizenship as revolutionary anti-violence. Within conditions of generalized cruelty, we can only *oppose* violence by *facing up* to the forms of extreme violence all around us. This means that in our world of colonial-racial capitalism, which keeps the vast majority of the planet in conditions of bare survival and instrumentality, *there is no other form of truly political action than the constant rupture of the atmosphere of violence with insurrectional activity that counters cruelty with civility*. And if insurrection is the "active" modality of citizenship,[52] then being a citizen can mean nothing other than taking part in the ongoing struggle against all forms of cruelty—that is, *undertaking permanent revolutionary action in the name of a new humanity*. While Arendt might have mocked Fanon for claiming that life is a constant struggle, his call for revolutionary anti-violence is, above all, a call to overcome the systemic cruelty that turns life itself into a struggle for so many through a struggle for freedom, equality, and justice for all. To us, there has never been a more radical call for a *new beginning* than the conclusion to *The Wretched of the Earth*. It is a call to every person who picks up that book, understands it, and, hopefully, hears it. The reader is not to simply put it down and pick up another, but to join the struggle for a new humanity. I have been so insistent that we look more carefully at the nuances of what gets called "violence" in political philosophy because without these nuances there is only a simplistic condemnation of the revolutionary action that is beginning to take place on our streets. I therefore hope that my contribution here might make it all the more possible to truly heed Fanon's call:

[I]f we want humanity to take one step forward, if we want to take it to another level than the one where Europe has placed it, then we must innovate, we must be pioneers. . . . For Europe, for ourselves, and for humanity, comrades, we must make a new start, develop a new way of thinking, and endeavor to create a new humanity.[53]

Chapter 2

The Struggle in Process
On Revolution and Black Liberation

CREATIVE REVOLUTION

We all supposedly know what The Revolution looks like. Men in military uniforms stride triumphantly into the central square of the capital city, the palaces of government are seized, the vestiges of the *ancien régime* are summarily disposed, members of the old guard are exiled or executed, streets are renamed, statues to the Great Leaders are built. And then the Terror begins: revolutionary fervor gives way to paranoia as the Party starts to devour its own, and the utopian dream becomes an authoritarian nightmare as increasingly ruthless measures are needed to preserve what has been won and all forms of brutal repression become justified in the name of The Revolution. In the Euro-American political imaginary, revolution always ends up looking more or less the same: it looks like France in 1789, Russia in 1917, China in 1949, maybe even Cuba in 1959. And by omission, we also know what revolution does not look like: it is apparently not Haiti, Tanzania, or South Africa, for instance. This imaginary of revolution is shared equally by those thinkers who would warn against it and those who dream of it. It is what Wendy Brown has in mind when she refers to revolution as "unquestionably finished," a relic of the twentieth century that the Left must find a way to mourn without nostalgia or melancholia,[1] and it is what Alain Badiou imagines when he writes of revolution as a hypothetical "event."[2] If Brown implores us to recuperate utopia without "the mechanism of revolution" and Badiou calls for a revolutionary "fidelity" to a specific series of Big Events (namely: the Paris Commune, the Russian Revolution, the Chinese Cultural Revolution, and May '68), it is because they both, like most Euro-American political theorists, assume we already know what revolution looks like—indeed, what revolution *is*.

This ontology of revolution as an "event" or as a distinct "modality" of politics purportedly shapes everything we know and imagine about revolution—even what we are *capable* of imagining. It is, so the story goes, what determines whether or not some believe that revolution is "still" possible, whether it is even desirable. It frames how what some European leftists think about the relationship between the spontaneous insurrectional activity and revolution discussed in the last chapter. About how particular struggles here and now can or cannot assume the universality of revolution. It makes us confident that we will know revolution when we see it, that we can tell whether this or that uprising is revolutionary. And with our gaze trained on the Big Idea of Revolution or on the Big Events of History, we overlook the transformative struggles taking place all around us: so sure that we know what revolution looks like, we either convince ourselves that it is something that can never happen again, not in what we call "today's world," or we dismiss ongoing revolutionary action because it does not look like the Big Event we are waiting for. And we therefore fail to see that revolutionary action—what it is and what we imagine it could be—is constantly changing in the very process of people's struggles.

In this chapter, I will argue that to think revolution as a continual struggle for a new way of being human, we need a different political imaginary—one that imagines revolution not as a Big Event but as a *creative process*, not as a "mechanism" of transformation but as *transformation itself*. Fanon as we saw hoped for as much while recognizing the trauma of the struggle against decolonization but held on to the possibility of what the philosopher Lewis Gordon called "liberation for." Gordon makes a distinction between "liberation for" and "liberation from." To quote Gordon, "Liberation from is a response to harm; liberation for is for is the rallying call of creative resources of possibility."[3]

In the last chapter we saw how the horror of the dehumanization of the colonized blocks political life. "Liberation against" is necessary for the return of politics. Again, to quote Gordon,

Under Euromodern rule, the harms of colonialism, enslavement required impositions of rule which barred politics in the lives upon those upon whom they were imposed. This was one of Steve Bantu Biko's insights on the South African apartheid state. To maintain itself it waged a war not only against non-white peoples but also against politics because to maintain its itself it had to prioritize rule at the expense of political life. Blocking politics required barring political life from certain groups of people. This involved making them invisible.[4]

The fight for visibility is part of what Fanon calls the "grandeur of spontaneity,"[5] but "liberation against" cannot provide us with decolonization and the revolutionary action it demands.[6] But let me be clear: I am not arguing against the idea that revolution might, indeed often must, involve both defensive and offensive armed struggles (which, again, I prefer to think of as *anti-violent action* against the cruelty of colonial-racial capitalism). Those who argue that revolution is a relic of the past might concede "liberation against" but deny the revolutionary possibility of "liberation for." This is why Gordon's distinction between the two kinds of liberation is so important. Why is it so crucial for Gordon that we stress the importance of "liberation for"? As he points out,

> We should remember that if we think of the work to be done simply as that of elimination, of reaction, to the right, our course could lead to a form of anarchy in which we become small, privatized protectorates—in short, again, a left that becomes the right. We need a responsible form of practice attuned to the many dimensions of what we are and our relationship to other forms of life. We need to unleash our capacity to create, to build meaning, while being sober to the realities of the terrestrial creatures we are. This requires not only a shift in the geography of reason but also an understanding of the fragility of life in its wider context.[7]

As I will stress in the next chapter, I am not against the idea that the creative force of people in struggle, which I identify with revolution itself, must be *organized*, even into party and state forms. I am certainly not arguing against the idea that a central aim of revolution is to seize political power and establish a government of the people, that the economic system must be completely reorganized away from the horrific exploitation inherent to all forms of capitalism, and that the ultimate goal of any revolutionary struggle is planetary socialism. What I am opposing, however, is the idea that there is a certain way of undertaking revolution based on how it has looked in the past, that the exemplars of revolution are four Big Events in Europe, and that that the so-called failures of mass uprisings to seize hegemony somehow proves that they are not truly revolutionary. And I want to strongly argue against the idea that the ideals of freedom, dignity, and justice can ever be separated from the "mechanism" of revolution.

To make this argument, I will turn to two of the most profound thinkers of what we might call *creative revolution*: Rosa Luxemburg and C. L. R. James. Over a century ago, Luxemburg famously wrote against any formulaic conception of socialist revolution, such as that she attributed to the Bolsheviks, insisting that the future to which revolutionary struggle aims can only be *created in the process of struggle itself*:

> The tacit assumption underlying the Lenin-Trotsky theory of dictatorship is this: that the socialist transformation is something for which a readymade formula lies completed in the pocket of the revolutionary party, which needs only to be carried out energetically in practice. That is, unfortunately—or perhaps fortunately—not the case. Far from being a sum of ready-made prescriptions which have only to be applied, the practical realization of socialism as an economic, social and juridical system is something which lies completely hidden in the mists of the future. What we possess in our program is nothing but a few main signposts which indicate the general direction in which to look for the necessary measures, and the indications are mainly negative in character at that. Thus we know more or less what we must eliminate at the outset in order to free the road for a socialist economy. But when it comes to the nature of the thousand, practical measures, large and small, necessary to introduce socialist principles into economy, law, and all social relationships, there is no key in any socialist party program or textbook. This is not a shortcoming but rather the very thing that makes scientific socialism superior to the utopian varieties.[8]

While we often know what we are struggling against and the wrongs we must struggle to right, a socialist future is not some sort of Platonic Ideal and revolution is not merely a mechanism for attaining it. Indeed, in a way that resonates with Henri Bergson's own rethinking of evolution away from mechanistic biology in *Creative Evolution* (1907),[9] Luxemburg actually understands revolution in terms of the open-ended creativity inherent to life itself:

The socialist system of society should be, and can only be, an historical product, born out of the school of its own experiences, born in the course of its realization, as a result of the developments of living history, which—just like organic nature of which, in the last analysis, it forms a part—has the fine habit of always producing along with any real social need the means to its satisfaction, along with the task simultaneously the solution. However, if such is the case, then it is clear that socialism by its very nature cannot be decreed or introduced by *ukase*. It has as its prerequisite a number of measures of force—against property, etc. The negative, the tearing down, can be decreed; the building up, the positive, cannot. New Territory. A thousand problems. Only experience is capable of correcting and opening new ways. Only unobstructed, effervescing life falls into a thousand new forms and improvisations, brings to light creative new force, itself corrects all mistaken attempts. . . . The whole mass of people must take part in it. Otherwise, socialism will be decreed from behind a few official desks by a dozen intellectuals.[10]

If evolution is the creative force of life itself—propelling life from form to form, always making life differ from itself, "correcting" it, and opening it to a future that is other—then we might call revolution *humanity's creative impulse*: the force or momentum by which people in struggle ceaselessly propel humanity toward a different future, ever striving to bring a new humanity into being. And in this way, revolution can never be reduced to either a "fidelity" to the past or to a program—even a hypothesis—that can capture the future for, like evolution, what revolution "is" at any given time is itself in a process of becoming as deep and ongoing as the concrete forms of struggle to which this creative impulse gives rise.

While for Luxemburg, the notion of revolution is a creative impulse inherent to people in struggle, I want to take one step beyond her to explicitly focus on the importance of the imagination.[11] As Immanuel Kant famously taught us, scientific laws are postulates of theoretical reason, and where theoretical reason ends, the *imagination begins*. This was Kant's way of preserving freedom in the then-new deterministic universe of Newtonian mechanics: that we can never *know* we are bound by causal laws is what opens the space for imaginative freedom.[12] Herbert Marcuse has turned our attention to the great significance of this argument and its revolutionary legacy when he pointed out that without the imagination, there would be no way to move from a theoretical critique of actually-existing exploitation to the possibility of something *other*.[13] Through critique, we can identify the limitations imposed upon us and thereby come to adequately know what we are up against. But the future can never be *known*, it can only be imagined and created. It is for this reason that Orlando Patterson has suggested that it could only have been slaves who *imagined and created* freedom:[14] enslaved people who could not *know* what freedom "is," but who, through a critique of the limits imposed by their enslavement came both to know what had to be overcome and to *imagine* an otherwise that they called "freedom"—an otherwise that is still in creation, always yet to come, as people continue to struggle to bring it into being, a struggle that thus continually changes what socialism is and what we imagine it could be. Revolution is therefore a continual interplay—we could even call it a "dialectic"—between the materiality of struggle and the imagination: the future to which the struggle aims can only be imagined and never known in advance, but our imagination of what is possible changes in the very struggle itself as we, together, overcome the limits that have been imposed on us and learn how to live with one another in the world in a different way.[15] Or, as Étienne Balibar has beautifully phrased it, revolution "is a transformation of the past into a future that had not been imaginable."[16] But this means that revolution, even creative revolution, is as irreducible to any notion of scientific materialism as it is inseparable from what I have elsewhere called the indestructible *spirit* of revolution.[17] What revolution "is" is created, again and again, by people in struggle who transform both who they are and what they imagine that they could become. Any future beyond colonial-racial capitalism and the limits of the knowable that it imposes on us—beyond the dead ends of man[18]—will therefore only be brought into being by the creative power of people as they imagine it in the struggle for it.

ROSA LUXEMBURG AND THE SCHOOL OF STRUGGLE

Rosa Luxemburg's lifetime of participation in, and her deep and profound grappling with, all the complexities of revolutionary struggles speak directly to the relationship between what I am calling spontaneous insurrectional activity and revolution. Indeed, it is the unique emphasis Luxemburg places on spontaneity that sets her writings on revolutionary action considerably apart from her other comrades who sought to theorize revolution. In *The Mass Strike, the Political Party, and the Trade Unions* (1906), Luxemburg powerfully contrasts her own understanding of the "mass strike" with the traditional—and much more limited—notion of the general strike as a single, well-organized uprising by the industrial proletariat guided by the party leaders and the trade unions with the aim of seizing state power. As Luxemburg demonstrates with reference to the revolutionary struggles in Russia, however, the reality of mass uprisings cannot easily be grasped by such theoretical formulas:

> Now when we compare this theoretical scheme with the real mass strike as it appeared in Russia five years ago, we are compelled to say that this representation which, in the German discussion, occupies the central position, hardly corresponds to a single one of the many mass strikes that have taken place, and on the other hand, that the mass strike in Russia displays such a multiplicity of the most varied forms of action that it is altogether impossible to speak of "the" mass strike, of an abstract mass strike. All the factors of the mass strike, as well as its character, are not only different in the different towns and districts of the country, but its general character has often changed in the course of the revolution. The mass strike has passed through a definite history in Russia and is passing still further through it. Who, therefore, speaks of the mass strike in Russia must, above all things, keep its history before his eyes.[19]

Luxemburg illustrates her original understanding of the power of spontaneity in struggle with the example of the revolution in Russia in 1905, which, although it began as a strike over fired workers in one factory, quickly expanded far beyond even a general strike in the name of economic reform. After a month-long general strike across the factories of St. Petersburg had completely shut the city down, thousands marched on the Winter Palace on January 22, 1905, to deliver a petition to the Tsar demanding an improvement in working conditions but also an end to the Russo-Japanese War and universal suffrage.[20] As we know, the Tsar's armed forces responded to the demonstrations with the most severe repression, killing hundreds of protestors in one of the many tragic events known to history as "Bloody Sunday." And yet, this brutal reaction did not quell the mass movement; instead, it spread across the Russian Empire, not only to the cities from Moscow and Warsaw to Riga, Tbilisi, and Baku, where hundreds of thousands of workers participated in strike after strike, but also to peasant revolts in the countryside and within a year had led to the establishment of the Duma and the new constitution which brought an end to the Tsar's absolute rule. But despite the momentous *event* that the January uprising constituted, Luxemburg stressed that it must not be separated from the series of smaller strikes and insurrections over the previous years and, indeed, the general strike in St. Petersburg in 1896, for even despite their so-called failures and the intervening periods without insurrectional activity, these were all essential to the *continuing* struggle toward democratic socialism in Russia. To quote Luxemburg as she defends the importance of the 1896 strike against those who dismissed it as an isolated demand for wages in the textile factories rather than a properly "political" revolution:

> [T]he strike [of 1896] was outwardly a mere economic struggle for wages, but the attitude of the government and the agitation of the Social Democracy made it a political phenomenon of the first rank. The strike was suppressed; the workers suffered a "defeat." But in January of the following year, the textile workers of St Petersburg repeated the general strike once more and achieved this time a remarkable success: the legal introduction of a working day of eleven hours throughout the whole of Russia. What was nevertheless a much more important result was this: since that first general strike of 1896 which was entered upon without a trace of organization or of strike funds, an intensive trade union fight began in Russia proper which spread from St. Petersburg to the other parts of the country and opened up entirely new vistas to Social Democratic agitation and organization, and by which in the apparently death-like peace of the following period the revolution was prepared by underground work.[21]

This point is extremely important in understanding how Luxemburg's thinking of the mass strike differs sharply from other theories of how spontaneous insurrectional activity becomes revolutionary. Workers—and, of course, in our post-industrial times, we would have to extend this category to all of those dispossessed and exploited by global capitalism—learn, *in the course of their struggles*, important lessons about organization, about staying power, about the economic and political causes of their exploitation, and, ultimately, about the socialist future they are fighting for. In struggle, as Luxemburg puts it, new vistas are opened that forever transform people's sense of what is possible. For

Luxemburg, then, revolution is not an "event" but a continuous process of transformation that may seem uneven—and, indeed, may sometimes seem to have "disappeared" from one major insurrection to the next. But what she shows us is that the real lessons of revolution are those that are learned in struggle itself and, in that way, the revolutionary process steadily advances toward a deeper, more critical understanding of capitalism and a richer imagination of democratic socialism. Even when it does not look like anything is "happening," revolutionary transformations are taking shape both individually and collectively. Indeed, these transformations often take place so rapidly that they remain imperceptible to theorists and party leaders habituated to looking only for widescale, well-organized, disciplined industrial action. Again, to quote Luxemburg on the aftermath of the 1905 uprisings:

> Everywhere at that time the Social Democratic organizations went ahead with appeals; everywhere revolutionary solidarity with the St. Petersburg proletariat was expressly stated as the cause and aim of the general strike; everywhere, at the same time, there were demonstrations, speeches, conflicts with the military. But even here there was no predetermined plan, no organized action, because the appeals of the parties could scarcely keep pace with the spontaneous risings of the masses; the leaders had scarcely time to formulate the watchwords of the onrushing crowd of the proletariat.[22]

Spontaneous insurrectional activity should therefore never be reduced to some party platform, let alone some party's conception of what is "true" about how The Revolution can and must take place. This is why Luxemburg challenges the idea that revolution springs fully formed from a united proletariat driven by clearly enumerated political goals and a "properly" revolutionary subjectivity instilled in them by the party leaders and unions. She illustrates this by pointing out the myriad of revolutionary transformations that had to happen in both individuals and collectives before the event that came to be called the Russian Revolution could ever become possible. And far from non-political, or simply an aside to The Revolution, these continuing transformations are themselves the very materiality of struggle, the creative force and momentum of revolutionary action:

> Absolutism cannot be overthrown at any desired moment in which only adequate "exertion" and "endurance" are necessary. The fall of absolutism

is merely the outer expression of the inner social and class development of Russian society. Before absolutism can, and may be overthrown, the bourgeois Russia must be formed in its interior, in its modern class divisions. That requires the drawing together of the various social layers and interests, besides the education of the proletarian revolutionary parties, not less of the liberal, radical, petit-bourgeois, conservative and reactionary parties; it requires the self-consciousness, self-knowledge, and the class consciousness not merely of the layers of the people, but also of the layers of the bourgeoisie. But this also can be achieved and come to fruition in no way but in the struggle, in the process of revolution itself, through the actual school of experience, in collision with the proletariat as well as with one another, in incessant mutual friction.[23]

While this passage might seem to be riddled with the outdated class language of her time, Luxemburg's argument here goes to the very heart of how we are to understand the importance of spontaneous insurrectional activity to revolution. As she sees it, in their disregard of spontaneity, party organizations often fail to see the revolution that is in process right in front of them as an organized movement emerges *from* the activity of the people: "And finally another thing, the apparently 'chaotic' strikes and the 'disorganized' revolutionary action after the January [1905] general strike is becoming the starting point of a feverish *work of organization*."[24] Luxemburg's central point, then, is that the workers themselves, in the course of their spontaneous activity, constitute the force that propels revolution onward both as they increase the organization of their insurrectional action and as they develop a political understanding of the crisis to which their actions are responding. Each one of the strikes in Russia thus built off of and carried forward those prior to it as the workers learned step-by-step what they were politically up against. Indeed, this is one of Luxemburg's key insights: the "mass strike" is not something that simply "happens" and then peters out. It is a continuous force that comes in waves. "It is absurd to think," she writes, "of the mass strike as one act, one isolated action. The mass strike is rather the indication, the rallying idea, of a whole period of the class struggle lasting for years, perhaps decades."[25]

Luxemburg's analysis of the strikes in Russia also help to understand that the economic and the political can never be neatly separated in revolutionary struggle. What in 1896 began as a strike for an eleven-hour workday, for instance, became a political movement that resulted in legal reforms. For Luxemburg, the separation of the economic and the political as a fundamental divide that must be manipulated by party leaders so as to push the proletariat to the next stage of the Revolution completely misunderstands the waves of revolutionary struggle that she alerts us to. There is, on the contrary, a constant *relay* between the economic and the political because struggles that appear to be purely economic—about the workday or wages, for example—move quickly to challenge state authority that can either respond to their demands with reform or retaliate with the worst kinds of violence and cruelty. Indeed, for Luxemburg, the conceptual cleaving of the economic and the political is yet another way in which revolutionary theorists not only fail to grasp the ongoing struggle in process, but actually threaten to paralyze it:

> In a word, the economic struggle is the transmitter from one political center to another; the political struggle is the periodic fertilization of the soil for the economic struggle. Cause and effect here continually change places; and thus the economic and the political factor in the period of the mass strike, now widely removed, completely separated or even mutually exclusive, as the theoretical plan would have them, merely form the two interlacing sides of the proletarian class struggle in Russia. And, *their unity is precisely the mass strike*. If the sophisticated theory purposes to make a clever logical dissection of the mass strike for the purpose of getting at the "purely political mass strike," it will by this dissection, as with any other, not perceive the phenomenon in its living essence, but will kill it altogether.[26]

We know that the mass uprising in 1905 did not succeed in seizing state power. And this fact will go on to have an enormous impact on how party organization was rethought throughout the European revolutionary parties—particularly by the Bolsheviks who traced the so-called failure of the 1905 Revolution to the masses not fully understanding their revolutionary task, which therefore demonstrated the need for a tight central committee that would assume responsibility for that task. Luxemburg, for her part, was a profound believer in the revolutionary party and her disagreement with Lenin, to which I will return in the next chapter, was not over such a need but rather the *kind* of party that should be formed. But more important for our purposes here is Luxemburg's insistence that spontaneous insurrectional activity can never be programmed in advance or led in any kind of neat and precise "scientific" manner. Instead, a revolutionary party must be able to read the language of the struggle itself and to learn new lessons from the people about what revolution looks like and why and how it is possible. The party does not stand above the "masses" as some kind of elite that knows the truth and gets it right, and revolutionary intellectuals do not sit on the sidelines and lecture as if they were in a classroom of ignorant people who do not understand the significance of their own actions. On the contrary, it is how the people in struggle understand and imagine their own actions and the future they are fighting for that the revolutionary party and intellectuals must learn in order to even begin to think about what it might mean to "lead." As Luxemburg puts it, the self-proclaimed revolutionary leader often "fails to see that the only subject to whom the role of controller now falls is the *mass ego* of the working class that everywhere insists on making its own mistakes and learning the dialectic of history for itself."[27] And as her own life shows us, even the best and brightest of revolutionary comrades need to constantly learn new languages, new ideas, new rituals, and new practices from the school of struggle.

C. L. R. JAMES AND THE BLACK REVOLUTIONARY LEGACY

The long legacy of struggles for Black liberation and decolonization has produced some of the most creative practices of revolution as they bequeath to humanity a much richer understanding of the past and present of capitalist exploitation and vivid reimaginations of the future we are fighting for. Of course, many "traditional" Marxist-Leninist thinkers remain steadfastly devoted to the idiom of industrial class politics and see issues of racism and colonization as secondary, if not as "distractions" from the universality of the struggle for socialism. It is for this reason that many Black and decolonial radicals have abandoned Marxist revolutionary theory as a tool for conceptualizing their own struggles. But as many Black comrades—from Angela Davis to Frantz Fanon, from Kwame Nkrumah to Chris Hani—have shown, the struggle for Black liberation and decolonization is inseparable from the struggle for socialism. Indeed, a central argument of this book is that Black liberation and decolonization *are* struggles for socialism imagined precisely as a *new collective praxis of being human*. Few thinkers have written more powerfully on Black struggles as revolutionary struggles for socialism than C. L. R. James. Like Luxemburg, James argued that we have to turn to people themselves whose creativity in struggle is what allows for truly revolutionary thought and action. And, like Luxemburg, James's writings are always attempts to grapple with his own experiences in revolutionary activism—in his case Trotskyism—and the limits of the traditional party orthodoxies. I will return to James's critique of the vanguard party and his rethinking of dialectical materialism later in this book, but here I want to emphasize how James's reflections on the way in which spontaneous insurrectional activity creates its own organization and leadership, rather than the organized party leadership creating the movement, offers a reimagination of revolution as a creative process.

As with Luxemburg's rereading of the Russian Revolution of 1905, some of James's most important writings on this subject focus on the US Civil Rights Movement. In his thoughts on Martin Luther King Jr., James demonstrates how King—like the majority of Black people in Montgomery, Alabama, during the famous strike against the bus companies—was educated on the significance of the movement only in what Luxemburg calls the "school of experience" itself. As is well-known, the bus boycott began in 1955 after Rosa Parks was arrested for refusing to give up her seat to a white man and move to the back of the bus. While the local NAACP had been planning action against segregation for some time and thus the action was not entirely "spontaneous," the magnitude of the insurrection, like the initial strike in St. Petersburg in December 1904, is something that could never have been predicted by any organizational leadership. As James describes the immediate aftermath of Parks's arrest:

> The news spread, and on the Monday morning there began one of the most astonishing events in the history of human struggle. The negro population of Montgomery is about 35,000. From the Monday morning and for about one year afterwards, the percentage of negroes who boycotted the buses was over 99%. The Commissioner of Police and the head of the bus company have stated that never on any day did more than 46 people ride the buses.[28]

The boycott was such a tremendous, but unpredicted, success that a committee was called about where to go from there. King, then a 26-year-old preacher, was selected to head the action committee, but King did not assume this role on the basis of some orthodox theory or predetermined political program by which he would lead the "masses." Rather, the very principles that would come to guide the entire Civil Rights Movement emerged from King's reflections on the struggle itself:

> King, who had been elected chairman of the committee, left the company and went outside for half an hour's meditation. He recognized that this movement had to have some political policy to guide it. He had no idea whatever of being a leader for the struggles of his people. He was a young man of 28 [sic] years, but he had read philosophy and he had also read the writings of Gandhi, but with no specific purpose in view. In the course of the half hour's meditation, however, the idea came to him that what was needed to give this movement a social and political underpinning was the policy of nonviolence. But as he explained, nonviolence as he conceived it, had nothing passive about it. While it stopped short at armed rebellion, it is incessantly active in its attempt to impress its determination and the strength of its demands upon those upon whom it is directed.[29]

The "policy" of non-violent action in the Civil Rights Movement, as I argued in the previous chapter, should not be taken as some kind of metaphysical principle. As James shows us here, it was an idea that came to King from within the overwhelming and unexpected success of the Montgomery bus strike as a way of organizing the force of the spontaneous insurrectional activity into the forward momentum of what was to quickly become a revolutionary struggle sweeping throughout the country. More importantly, James's point here is one that brings us back to Luxemburg and the central argument of this chapter: King was *educated by the process of struggle*. His leadership emerged from the creative impulse unleashed by that historical strike; he did not guide the movement from "above." James's reflections on King go to his larger defense of what came to be known as the Civil Rights Movement as a *revolutionary* struggle, although it has often been depicted as the very exemplar of a reformist movement. Indeed, already by 1957 James had recognized the emerging Black movements in the US as developing a new vocabulary and practice of revolution—one that his white Euro-American comrades were at risk of overlooking:

The revolutionary movement on the whole and the Marxist movement in particular will be making a fundamental mistake, (i) if it does not recognize these movements for what they are, a form of revolutionary struggle characteristic of our age; (ii) if we allow ourselves to be misled by this label of non-violence which they have pasted upon it, which can cause a lot of confusion unless we look beyond the surface and see the tremendous boldness, the strategic grasp, and the tactical inventiveness, all of these fundamentally revolutionary, with which they handled it.[30]

For James, what is most significant in the Civil Rights Movement is what it shared with other revolutionary movements taking place throughout the world at that time that demonstrate the creative power of people in struggle, namely the movement for independence in Ghana and the Hungarian Revolution. Once again, like Luxemburg, James's stress is on the force of the people's spontaneous insurrectional activity in *creating* revolution. Revolution does not begin when the party leader pushes the "masses" to assume their ordained revolutionary task. Beneath the surface of what might appear like waves of inaction and chaotic spontaneity, revolution is already underway in the people's *transformations on themselves*. To quote James:

> The conclusion to be drawn at the general level of the mass movement in both advanced and backward countries, particularly since the end of World War II, is such that they recognize immediately any leadership which is saying that thing that they want to hear. There is no need for any preparation. I hope no-one underestimates the tremendous inner power of a movement which results in 99% of the population refusing to ride in the buses for over a whole year. . . . It is one of the most astonishing events of endurance by a whole population that I have ever heard of. The movements of the people in the Gold Coast, Montgomery, and the Hungarian Revolution is a warning to all revolutionaries not to underestimate the readiness of modern people everywhere to overthrow the old regime.[31]

As a committed Marxist, James believed in the ultimate need to unite movements of African Americans and African decolonization with the industrial proletariat. But as a Black man himself his emphasis was always on the need for white revolutionaries to understand the revolutionary power of Black struggles. James made this point in "The Revolutionary Answer to the Negro Problem in the US," which was presented at the Socialist Workers Party Convention in 1948 where

James argued forcefully against the prevailing idea that the Black movement is revolutionary only insofar as it is brought under the leadership of the labor movement:

> We say, number 1, that the Negro struggle, the independent Negro struggle, has avitality and a validity of its own; that it has deep historic roots in the past of America and in present struggles; it has an organic political perspective, along which it is traveling, to one degree or another, and everything shows that at the present time it is traveling with great speed and vigor.
>
> We say, number 2, that this independent Negro movement is able to intervene with terrific force upon the general social and political life of the nation, despite the fact that it is waged under the banner of democratic rights, and is not led necessarily either by the organized labor movement or the Marxist party.
>
> We say, number 3, and this is the most important, that it is able to exercise a powerful influence upon the revolutionary proletariat, that it has got a great contribution to make to the development of the proletariat in the United States, and that it is in itself a constituent part of the struggle for socialism.[32]

At the Dialectics of Liberation Congress in London in 1967, James went even further in defending the emerging Black Power movement not merely as one subpart of the proletariat, but the very *vanguard* of US revolutionary politics: "The kind of impact the Negroes are making," James writes, "is due to the fact that they constitute a vanguard not only to the Third World, but constitute also that section of the United States which is most politically advanced."[33] This is why James argued that it is not for critics and theorists to dictate which strategies and tactics Black movements should adopt, for it is the people in struggle—and they alone—who determine the shape of revolution as they propel the movement onward:

> Who are we to say, "Yes, you are entitled to say this but not to say that; you are entitled to do this but not to do that?" If we know the realities of Negro oppression in the USA (and if we don't we should keep our mouths shut until we do), then we should guide ourselves by a West Indian expression which I recommend to you: *what he do, he well do*. Let me repeat that: what the American Negroes do is, as far as we are concerned,

well done. They will take their chances, they will risk their liberty, they risk their lives if need be. *The decisions are theirs.*[34]

For James, then—and against the completely opposite view of "traditional" Marxist intellectuals—Black struggles in the US have what he understands as a vanguard role in inspiring all others to revolutionary action:

> It was the Black people beginning with the agitation in Montgomery, Alabama which started what was known as the New Left Movement. ... What matters is that these events took place and came to the attention of many people who are not readers of books but are moved by events. It demonstrated that a great political movement was taking place in the sense of what was actually happening and the possibilities opening up for future developments in the population.[35]

James's analysis of Black movements in the US demonstrates how seemingly isolated events of "spontaneous" insurrectional activity actually cohere into a global revolutionary movement. In *Nkrumah and the Ghana Revolution* (1977), for instance, he writes of how spontaneous uprisings in Harlem in 1943—not unlike the St. Petersburg textile strike of 1896—unleashed a revolutionary impulse that fed directly into the rising struggles for African decolonization:

> It is a social and political force which seems to grow in power and refinement of expression, as the people of the world, and with them Africans and people of African descent, break down the barriers to racial equality. Thus in Harlem, New York, in 1943, the Negroes broke out in a long-smoldering resentment against segregation and discrimination in general, and against high prices and the brutal treatment of black soldiers in Southern camps in particular. With a systematic and relentless thoroughness they smashed the windows of every shop owned by a white man throughout the area, and it is an established fact that those who did the smashing did not loot—the looting came after and was done by the poor and the hungry and the lumpen-proletarians who could not resist the sight of goods waiting to be taken. But what was most remarkable was that though tens of thousands were in the streets participating or sympathizing and encouraging, no single black person attempted any violence to any white person and crowds of white people, many of them from Manhattan, walked, watching and very often talking and exchanging cigarettes and lights with the Negroes in the most amicable manner.

The racial consciousness which has been so mercilessly injected into the Negro is today a source of action and at the same time of discipline.[36]

For James it is therefore a mistake to think of spontaneous insurrections as undisciplined and chaotic to the point where they are not even capable of making principled decisions about what kind of property is to be destroyed. In a way that echoes Luxemburg yet again, James here demonstrates that forms of political discipline and organization are *inherent* to what are often dismissed as "riots." There was discipline here. The violence was explicitly directed against white property, not people. This turns us again to the need for a new nuanced conception of violence I developed in chapter 1. Sure, when you are unable to get a job, let alone a decent one, you might be tempted to loot so that your family might survive for the next week; but as this description of the 1943 uprisings in Harlem attests, we must distinguish organized attacks on white property from looting.

But even more importantly, James here alerts us to an even bigger mistake on the part of revolutionary intellectuals: the failure to recognize that events of Black insurrectional action are vectors of *universal* revolutionary struggle. In his "Black Power" speech from 1967, James rejects the idea that the emphasis on *Blackness* in the Black Power movement, as opposed to the more general language of "civil rights," represents some sort of retrograde embrace of "cultural" or "racial" particularity:

> To too many people here in England, and unfortunately to people in the United States too . . . too many people see Black Power and its advocates as some kind of portent, a sudden apparition, as some racist eruption from the depths of black oppression and black backwardness. It is nothing of the kind. It represents the *high peak* of thought on the Negro question which has been going on for over half a century. That much we have to know, and that much we have to be certain other people get to know.[37]

Indeed, for James, insofar as Black struggles necessarily challenge the distribution of property within colonial-racial capitalism that systematically dispossesses Black people, these struggles should be seen as inherently *socialist*. As James writes of Stokely Carmichael:

> In the opinion of myself and many of my friends no clearer or stronger voice for socialism has ever been raised in the US. It is obvious that for

[Carmichael], based as he is and fighting for a future of freedom for the Negro people of the US, the socialist society is not a hope, *not what we may hope*, but a *compelling necessity*.³⁸

The very reason why the vanguard actions of Black people in US cities and beyond could inspire the revolutionary movements that followed them—such as the New Left, the Women's Movement, the Gay Liberation Movement, and so on—the reason why James could write simultaneously about the bus boycott in Montgomery, the decolonial struggle in Ghana, and the Revolution in Hungary, is because the creative force of people who take up revolutionary possibility and turn it into action *always* expresses what James called, following Hegel, a *universality*. This is not the abstract universality of the proletariat as the "universal class" *to* which the "masses" must be led by a vanguard party to assume, but what James calls a *concrete universality* that explodes *from* the accumulated transformations of people in struggle:

> The process is molecular, day by day never resting, continuous. But at a certain stage, the continuity is interrupted. The molecular changes achieve a universality and explode into a new quality, a revolutionary change. Previous to the revolutionary explosion, the aims of the struggle can be posed in partial terms, possibility. It is the impossibility of continuing to do this that interrupts the continuity. The revolution, precisely because it is a revolution, demands all things for all men. It is an attempt to leap from the realm of objective necessity to the realm of objective freedom.³⁹

Black struggles, then, should never be reduced to "identity politics" aimed only at anti-Black racism that must find their universality in the greater proletarian struggle. Famously, this was Jean-Paul Sartre's critique of the *Négritude* movement as a sort of racist anti-racism that could never reach the universality of the proletariat in the struggle for a liberated humanity. For James, on the contrary, it is not up to Black people to "cast of their *négritude* for the sake of the Revolution,"⁴⁰ but rather, Black struggles unleash the creative force of revolution that calls to *all others* in struggling toward a universality that James would explicitly call *socialism* or that Fanon and Sylvia Wynter would call a *new praxis of humanity*.

THE CONTINUING STRUGGLE FOR A NEW HUMANITY

C. L. R. James's writings on Black struggles challenge us to reimagine what we take revolution to be: what we expect it to look like, what form we expect it to take, where and when we expect it to occur, and who we expect to lead it. Thus, in a profound sense, James's reflections on the Black revolutionary legacy within the US are a necessary "creolization" of Rosa Luxemburg's powerful but Eurocentric thinking about revolutionary transformation as propelled by waves of spontaneous insurrectional action.[41] I believe that James's and Luxemburg's understanding of revolution as the creative power of people in struggle is essential to thinking socialist revolution as a continual struggle for a new humanity and for making sense of the ongoing action taking place today. Are the mass uprisings that began with the lynching of George Floyd *revolutionary*? I understand the recent uprisings as instances of spontaneous insurrectional activity that began in the wake of yet another lynching of a Black man in the US, which is part of a long legacy of revolutionary Black struggles for a new way of being human beyond the cruelty of colonial-racial capitalism. And this takes us directly to Luxemburg's central point about the transmission of the revolutionary impulse through periods of "slumber" or even "failure." For the fact that these uprisings began in response to *lynching* turns us back to the "failures" of the first major attempt to undo systematic racism in the US during the period of Reconstruction. The great revolutionary thinker—and one of C. L. R. James's most brilliant readers—Paget Henry has recently reframed the history of Black struggles in terms of three Reconstructions: first, the rebuilding of the South in the immediate aftermath of the Civil War; second, the mass uprisings that grew out of the Civil Rights Movement, which challenged the institutionalization of segregation at all levels of US political, economic, and social life; and, finally, the uprisings and actions taking place in the last few years under the banner of Black Lives Matter. This "Third Reconstruction," to paraphrase Henry, stands on the shoulders of the previous two, first, by understanding police murders of Black people as part of the atmosphere of violence that has pervaded the US since the first slave was brought from Africa—or, to be more precise, since the conquest of 1492. It also links the specific reform demands that the current movement is making on government, such as defunding the police, to the demands made in the prior Reconstructions for the end of slavery and of institutional segregation. This demonstrates that Black struggles have always been what Luxemburg calls a "relay" between the economic and the political.[42] Thus, seeking to end police brutality through the demand for government investment in Black lives and communities follows directly from the demand for abolitionist democracy from the First Reconstruction[43]—a demand that, once again, James recognized as a demand for *socialism*:

> [T]he Negro struggles in the South are not merely a question of struggles of Negroes, important as those are. It is a question of the reorganization of the whole agricultural system in the United States, and therefore a matter for the proletarian revolution and the reorganization of society on socialist foundations.[44]

The ongoing insurrectional activity in the name of Black Lives Matter is therefore not simply spontaneous, isolated outrage about individual lynchings. It is part of a long, continuous struggle of Black people for their freedom, dignity, and humanity—a struggle that even if it seems to have gone "quiet," will rise again and again until revolutionary action brings an end to the horrific cruelty of colonial-racial capitalism.

The poetic renaming of the ongoing uprisings as a possible "Third Reconstruction" speaks to many of my arguments in this chapter. It attests to the importance of imagining and reimagining struggles, both to gain a deeper understanding of oppression and a more vivid sense of what is possible. The light that it shines on a continuity in history—a history of cruelty, yes, but also a history of revolution—is exactly what Luxemburg means when she speaks of the waves upon waves of struggle that go on for decades or, in this case, hundreds of years. We cannot, of course, predict where this struggle will take us, but situating it within the history of continuing revolution is crucial for being able to recognize that it will teach us lessons that we never expected to learn—to show us new languages and practices of struggle that we all must learn how to read so that the full extent of what we are witnessing and participating in is not lost in the so-called ebbs and flows of spontaneity. On the one hand, these lessons must be learned from past struggles as, for instance, the possible Third Reconstruction learns from its own history—from slave rebellions and the great Haitian Revolution, from the Civil Rights Movement and Black Power, from the struggles for decolonization in Africa. But grappling with the creative force of insurrectional activity demands that we all be open to learning again from the school of experience and to being humbled before what we thought was certain about revolution. What revolution *is* and the new humanity that it is struggling for have been forever changed by Black struggles as they transform our very imagination of what it might mean to be human in a socialist world. And this is where spontaneous insurrectional activity finds its revolutionary universality: not as a predefined class, idea, or mechanism, but as a *call* that goes out to *each and every one of us* to join the struggle for a new way of being human together. Perhaps more than any other comrade-thinkers, Rosa Luxemburg and C. L. R. James help us to understand that revolution is not an "event" that either "succeeds" or "fails"—and it is certainly not "lost" to history. It is a never-ending struggle for a new praxis of being human—for *socialism*—propelled by an indestructible force—I would call it a *spirit*—of creativity that carries it from insurrection to insurrection like waves in the sea. As I write, a new wave is cresting and, like any wave, it might be bound to "fall"—but not without carrying the revolutionary sea forward and only until the next wave rises up.

Chapter 3

The Spirit of Struggle
On Dialectical Materialism and Political Spirituality

THE RETURN OF THE NEED FOR THE PARTY?

The question of the party has returned to revolutionary politics in recent years in a major way. It should be said that if we look beyond the Euro-American context it has *always* remained an urgent question, especially in Africa and Latin America where struggles for decolonization and socialism have constantly demanded a confrontation with all the complexities of revolutionary organization. But, over the past decade, both the successes and failures of new parties such as Podemos in Spain and Syriza in Greece, as well as the coalitions around Jeremy Corbyn and Bernie Sanders, have brought the idea of a socialist party back to the forefront of Euro-American politics, demonstrating Jean and John Comaroff's argument that tomorrow's most pressing theoretical questions were being grappled with in the Global South yesterday.[1] The return of the party follows decades of it being off the scene for a number of reasons: from the long shadow of Stalinism and the serious failures with the major Communist parties to address problems of racism, sexism, and homophobia, to the neoliberal reconsolidation of politics that turned parties into corporations unable to pose any real democratic challenge to capitalism. This is why the major surges of insurrectional activity in the last fifty years, from May '68 to Occupy Wall Street, have eschewed the old party form in favor of notions of dispersed multitudes and headless swarms.

But despite the return of the party to the practice of politics, very few Euro-American theorists have given it much consideration. One notable exception is Jodi Dean's *Crowds and Party*, which strongly argues that without organization, insurrectional activity will never be able to overthrow capitalism. "Capitalists will not simply hand over control and ownership of the means of production," she rightly notes. "States will not just stop oppressing, arresting, and imprisoning those who resist them. A Left that eschews organizing for power will remain powerless. This is why we are talking about the party again."[2] Drawing on the insights of psychoanalysis, Dean remedies an inattention within traditional Marxist-Leninist conceptions of the party to the *affective* dimension of insurrectional activity. What the "crowd" allows, in a spontaneous uprising, is a "de-individualization," which allows us to break free of the individualizing subjectivities imposed on us by neoliberal capitalism. This, she thinks, is what the politics of the multitude and the swarm understand. But, for Dean, unless the "crowd" is organized into a *party*, with collective interest, it will never be able to turn the spontaneous activity into revolutionary seizure of power. I am sympathetic to this argument, and I wholeheartedly agree that revolutionary politics cannot be content with spontaneous acts of resistance without institutionalization. But I am also troubled by Dean's return to a Leninist conception of the Communist Party (read through Lacanian psychoanalysis and Slavoj Žižek) because I reject the attempt to capture the organizational possibility of spontaneous insurrectional activity in advance with a Theory of the Party. In order to rethink this question of revolutionary collectivity, I will begin with a review of what Lenin actually said about the Party and the context in which he said it. Lenin was advocating for a national vanguard party in Russia, which was obviously a very challenging enterprise in such a vast territory at a time when, needless to say, there was no such thing as a "network society." He was also arguing against the idea that there could be a reformist non-revolutionary faction within a revolutionary party. I will return to the specifics of Lenin's argument shortly. But the core of this chapter is devoted to C. L. R. James and, in particular, his incredible and rarely-read *Notes on Dialectics*. James is one of our greatest thinkers of revolutionary struggle in the twentieth century because, like Lenin and Luxemburg, his theoretical work is part and parcel of his lifelong involvement in revolutionary struggle. What I hope to show in this chapter, first, is that the debate about the party is not only not outdated since it is raised in nation after nation in the Global South but also that it is related, as both Luxemburg and James saw, to the necessity of radical democracy to any revolutionary practices even after the seizure of state power. But as important a theoretical issue as the party remains for revolutionary struggle, our bigger point in this chapter is to return to *Notes on Dialectics* and James's rethinking of dialectical materialism as a new model for how to think the relation between "theory" and "practice" and the kinds of self-transformation necessary to any revolutionary thought and practice which I have elsewhere named *political spirituality*.

REVISITING LENIN ON THE PARTY

It is important to remember that in *One Step Forward, Two Steps Back* (1904), Lenin was engaging in active polemics within the Russian Social Democratic Labour Party (RSDLP) that would soon give rise to the Bolsheviks. First and foremost was the debate that Lenin had with his former mentor Georgi Plekhanov and other RSDLP members who wanted to form a minority (Mensheviks) within the Party who thought it would be possible to establish democratic reforms sweeping enough to challenge the rule of capitalism. In other words, capitalism could wither away without revolutionary struggle. On the level of party organization, the argument was that any worker, student, or intellectual could join the Party without being affiliated with the party organization and therefore influence the party program to be passed at the Congress. In this sense, the problem for Lenin was that in order to consolidate a party, there had to be a program and a set of rules and principles for organization that would form the basis of an actual party capable of carrying out revolutionary politics throughout Russia. Key to that plan was an understanding that it was necessary to establish an all-Russia revolutionary newspaper and this was one of the key debates in the Congress that Lenin polemicizes. To quote Lenin:

> Our Party Congress was unique and unprecedented in the entire history of the Russian revolutionary movement. For the first time a secret revolutionary party succeeded in emerging from the darkness of underground

life into broad daylight, showing everyone the whole course and outcome of our internal Party struggle, the whole character of our Party and of each of its more or less noticeable components in matters of programme, tactics, and organisation. For the first time we succeeded in throwing off the traditions of circle looseness and revolutionary philistinism, in bringing together dozens of very different groups, many of which had been fiercely warring among themselves and had been linked solely by the force of an idea, and which were now prepared (in principle, that is) to sacrifice all their group aloofness and group independence for the sake of the great whole which we were for the first time actually creating—the Party. But in politics sacrifices are not obtained gratis, they have to be won in battle. The battle over the slaughter of organisations necessarily proved terribly fierce. The fresh breeze of free and open struggle blew into a gale. The gale swept away—and a very good thing that it did!—each and every remnant of all circle interests, sentiments, and traditions without exception, and for the first time created genuinely Party institutions.[3]

Lenin's rejection of the idea that there should be a minority within the Party that relinquished revolutionary politics is quite close to Luxemburg's own condemnation of Bernsteinists who also argued that capitalism could "self-correct" through reforms so sweeping that bourgeois democracy would overtake the need for revolution. Both Lenin and Luxemburg were therefore staunchly on the side that it is simply not the case that anything like democracy—that is, real democratic control by the people over the means of production and the state apparatus—could take place if there was not a revolution that would decisively end capitalism and ultimately demolish class-based society. In his writings on centralism, then, Lenin is engaging in the concrete polemics of an actual Party Congress in order to establish a party that could consolidate itself as the Party of the Russian Revolution. It is thus important to underscore in response to today's defenders of the centralist or vanguard party: Lenin always insisted that what he called "dialectical truth" is always concrete and never abstract. "One of the basic principles of dialectics," as Lenin himself put it, "is that there is no such thing as abstract truth, truth is always concrete. . . . And, one thing more, the great Hegelian dialectics should never be confused with the vulgar worldly wisdom so well expressed by the Italian saying: *mettere la coda dove non va il capo* (sticking in the tail where the head will not go through)."[4] So there is no master Theory of the Party in Lenin, and certainly not one that relies on an ontology of the "split subject" that explains why the so-called masses cannot, through their own creative and spontaneous action, organize themselves effectively into a revolution. Lenin, because of his own reliance on Hegel's dialectical philosophy, always saw the role of the party as inseparable from the spontaneous action of the people to create new forms of organization. Of course, the classic example for Lenin was the rising of the Soviets as a new form of organization that emerged out of the struggles of workers and peasants themselves. The party, in this sense—and to use more modern language—was to read the text of the struggle and to always put them within the political context of revolution. The wisdom of the masses carried through one insurrection after another led to what Lenin called the "stored up knowledge" that moved toward a greater and greater universality. Indeed, Lenin himself was taking the stored-up wisdom of the Paris Commune of 1848 and developing it into a conception of socialism—Communism—that the Commune brought into history. Again, Lenin's thought was profoundly influenced by how the actual struggles of people lead to a wisdom that then creates new ideals, and one such new ideal that grew out of what was taking place on the ground was what he called socialism. In what Lenin understands as socialism following the Commune, the transfer of power to a workers' state is such that, for the first time, the vast majority of workers and ultimately all of the formerly exploited proletariats would take control of the state apparatus and suppress all forms of capitalist exploitation. The state under socialism would not simply "wither away" precisely because it demanded the dictatorship of the proletariat in order to actively suppress the capitalist class. To quote Lenin:

> And the dictatorship of the proletariat, i.e., the organization of the vanguard of the oppressed as the ruling class for the purpose of suppressing the oppressors, cannot result merely in an expansion of democracy. Simultaneously with an immense expansion of democracy, which for the first time becomes democracy for the poor, democracy for the people, and not democracy for the money-bags, the dictatorship of the proletariat imposes a series of restrictions on the freedom of the oppressors, the exploiters, the capitalists. We must suppress them in order to free humanity from wage slavery, their resistance must be crushed by force; it is clear that there is no freedom and no democracy where there is suppression and where there is violence.[5]

In other words, the state, at this stage of socialism, is to suppress capitalist resistance so that workers can slowly come not only to arm themselves and overcome capitalist exploitation but also to gain literacy over all forms of government. The Commune had produced new forms of democratic practice that the world had never seen and Lenin theorizes about these new forms as the basis of his new definition of socialism. But it is only in the transition to *communism* that workers thoroughly take over running the state themselves and it is then that the state begins to wither away:

> Only in communist society, when the resistance of the capitalists have disappeared, when there are no classes (i.e., when there is no distinction between the members of society as regards their relation to the social means of production), only then "the state . . . ceases to exist," and "it becomes possible to speak of freedom."[6]

In the first stage of communism, to paraphrase Lenin, workers and peasants become state employees. They now govern both the economy and the political organizations and these new socialist forms of political organization begin the process in which "the state apparatus" as it has been organized in capitalist society withers away:

> From the moment all members of society, or at least the vast majority, have learned to administer the state themselves, have taken this work into their own hands, have organized control over the insignificant capitalist minority, over the gentry who wish to preserve their capitalist habits and over the workers who have been thoroughly corrupted by capitalism—from this moment the need for government of any kind begins to disappear altogether. The more complete the democracy, the nearer the moment when it becomes unnecessary. The more democratic the "state" which consists of the armed workers, and which is "no longer a state in the proper sense of the word," the more rapidly every form of state begins to wither away.[7]

In other words, it was Lenin who understood the lessons of stored-up wisdom from the Commune as mandating nothing less than that every worker and every cook would be capable of government. But, for Lenin, this would also demand an effort to achieve literacy on a level never known before in Russia under Tsardom and this would be possible as the other side of the workers' state that Lenin identified with socialism.

By reading the stored-up wisdom of the Commune and giving form to the content of the Commune through the creation of new forms of democratic participation, Lenin was following what the lessons of the Commune meant for understanding how revolution had been changed in its very meaning by what the Commune had accomplished before its brutal obliteration by the ruling class. Did Lenin defend the idea that the Party had a political role to play in releasing the spontaneity and creativity of the people? Yes, but in a very specific sense. We will now turn to C. L. R. James's own interpretation of Lenin's conception of the party and perhaps more importantly the role in Lenin of holding on to his work in *State and Revolution* as the universal definition of what socialism would seek to achieve.

THE SIGNIFICANCE OF C. L. R. JAMES'S REINTERPRETATION OF LENIN

As C. L. R. James explains in *Notes on Dialectics*:

> The history of the theory and practice of this unprecedented phenomenon in human history is the history of the proletarian political party. Lenin understood this, and would have laughed to scorn the idea that he was the originator of the "party." He saw the party as the proletariat's *means of knowing*. The struggle of political parties in bourgeois society was the ideal, which the actual struggle of classes would transform into reality. In a series of profoundly philosophical observations between 1907 and 1914 Lenin made it clear that the proletariat could have no knowledge of the relationship of forces in the state, i.e., the existing state of affairs, except through the activity of its political party. The bourgeoisie did not need this.[8]

This is a "vanguard" role in a very precise sense and, of course, Lenin was working within the concrete situation of a Russia that had not yet achieved bourgeois democracy, which meant that the capacity of the working class to organize itself for reform was limited. In such a country, the struggle might need a very different kind of party and Lenin was certainly aware that this might be the case. As James reminds us, Lenin's understanding of the party was tailored to a specific form of organization demanded by the concrete situation in Russia and the need to politically consolidate revolutionary possibility against a form of absolutism that crushed even the most limited bourgeois forms of democracy. There is a sense in which Lenin did not think that the divide between being and knowing could be overcome until the workers had actually achieved a workers' state within socialism. But the universal, which for Lenin only begins in *communism*, was as James puts it:

> The history of man is his effort to make the abstract universal concrete. He constantly seeks to destroy, to move aside, that is to say, to negate what impedes his movement towards freedom and happiness. Man is the subject of history. "(The) subject, (man) is pure and simple negativity." This is a cardinal principle of the dialectical movement. The process is molecular, day by day never resting, continuous. But at a certain stage, the continuity is interrupted. The molecular changes achieve a universality and explode into a new quality, a revolutionary change. Previous to the revolutionary explosion, the aims of the struggle can be posed in partial terms, possibility. It is the impossibility of continuing to do this that interrupts the continuity. The revolution, precisely because it is a revolution, demands all things for all men. It is an attempt to leap from the realm of objective necessity to the realm of objective freedom.[9]

So what would James say to those now calling for a return to "the Leninist Party" and to the division between a party that *knows* and the masses that *implement*—that is, to the divide between being and knowing? For Lenin it was clear that under communism, the Party would wither away with the state that had as its goal the suppression by force of capitalist relations of production. As James writes:

> This is *our* Universal—the question of the party. Lenin could only pose it by implication. I repeat. If every cook learnt to govern, if every worker to a man administered the economy of the state, then the party as knowing could not be in opposition to the proletariat as being. If in 1920 the proletariat as being did not have the tragic necessity of defending itself against the proletariat as knowing, then it would mean that the contradiction between the proletariat as being and knowing had been solved. The greatness of Lenin is that in the harsh realities of Russia, he administered on the basis of reality but never for a moment lost sight of, or let others lose sight of, his Universal.[10]

What was this Universal? For Lenin, it was the transition to communism, which I would agree with James would be the beginning of a new humanity—human beings that could, for the first time, create for themselves what it meant to be human.[11] With the end of capitalist oppression, the end of all enforced forms of inequality and the divide between being and knowing would come to an end. For James—and as I will discuss, he is working through the fundamental categories of Hegel's *Science of Logic*—the stored-up wisdom of revolution turns into the elaboration of new forms of not only theory but practices of how a revolution might actually be possible. What James took from Hegel is that empirical reality does not just come to us without mediation, but instead we know it only through our ideas and concepts of it, which themselves are then challenged by the way in which reality itself is always moving and changing. To quote James:

> Here again is the *empirical, material* basis of all Logic. *He* says that the categories *express* the world spirit. We say they express man's material practice. But he says what we can say. That piecemeal, by instinct, impulse, changing, etc., they come into the mind and we must organize them, once we recognize that they express some order.[12]

James wrote *Notes on Dialectics* at a time when he had dropped out of leadership in the Socialist Workers' Party and had rejected Trotskyism. Trotsky, for James, was caught in the categories of the Understanding that throw the concrete lessons of the Russian Revolution into static, theoretical generalizations. Simply put, for James, Trotsky was not a dialectical thinker. For James, the tragedy of the Russian Revolution was that the ideal of socialism laid out as a program of concrete contents of the workers' state could not be realized in Russia:

> The tragedy of the Russian revolution is that the programme could not be carried out. The glory of leninism—and the *greatest*, incomparably the greatest of all lessons for us, is that never, never for a single moment, did he ever lose sight of the programme. He made tactical compromises, but he kept the programme, the new Universal, concretely before the people. That is why that programme is, for us, the most concrete of guides *today*. But to see that is not easy. It is lost and *we have to revive it*. Just as the abstract ideas of Lenin's struggle for bourgeois democracy became the concrete struggle for the whole world, so the abstract ideas which Lenin so consciously held up before backward Soviet Russia have become the concrete basis for the most advanced societies of our day. It is from the individual, the concrete, that we get the abstractions which enrich the Notion, and give us that total vision without which we cannot see the

object, the reality. We have to hew our way through to this. We have to hew our way through the wall Trotsky has built between the Russian experience and Western Europe.[13]

State and Revolution was, to remind the reader, Lenin's attempt to think what socialism means following the lessons of the Paris Commune. James now seeks to clarify why Lenin's own articulation of the Universal is no longer adequate to what revolution demands today, and "today" not only means James's time but also our own. Again, to quote James:

> Lenin wrote *State and Revolution*. His task was to clarify the theory of the state and the relation of the workers to the state—the idea of the workers' state. From this Universal he drew this determination of the concrete relations. That is not, cannot be our task today. . . . We are beyond *State and Revolution*. I can summarize where we are in the phrase: *The Party and Revolution*. That is our leap. That is our new Universal—the abolition of the distinction between party and mass. In the advanced countries we are not far from it in actuality. When we wrote in *The Invading Socialist Society* that in ten years the population would be totally re-educated and made truly social (but this only through its own efforts), we were saying just that. But whatever the distance between Idea and Actuality, and it is never very great, because the Idea always comes from some actuality, we get this concept of the relation of party and mass into our heads or we remain on the outskirts of politics. This is the meaning of a Universal. This is the Absolute Idea, the concrete embodiment in thought of subject and object, of ideal and real, of politics and economics, of organization and spontaneity, of party and mass. Every cook, every worker, to a man, to administer the state and run the economy: that was 1917. Today every cook, every worker, to a man, to join the party, the revolutionary party, which today, not tomorrow, not after the revolution, but today will in its own ranks begin the destruction of the bureaucracy. If the gap between Universal and Actuality is as great as it was in Russia 1917 (it is most certainly not that), the theoretical necessity remains. Without it the fate of a contemporary revolutionary group is sealed.[14]

So, what lessons can we draw from James's profound "creolization" of Lenin? Lenin organized the party in particular circumstances in which the ideals of the Russian Revolution could not be realized due to the brutality of the war that was unleashed against the Bolsheviks, the terrible starvation of masses of people, and the desperate effort put in to simply surviving. We can honor Lenin for holding onto the universal as he understood socialism as an armed workers' state and the need to suppress the oppressors, but for James, Lenin's refusal to relinquish the ideal of communism was the beginning of being human together in a new way. To quote James:

> Socialist society would sublate this revolutionary essence of capital and enrich *humanity* within it. Man, by becoming revolutionary, continuously active and creative, would become truly human. The real history of *humanity* would begin. Politics would be replaced by the administration of things. The difference between manual and intellectual labour would vanish. We must remember these phrases. Man would become truly man by the release of his human function—*creative action in labour*. The difference between being and knowing as separate functions would vanish. Man would know only by his creative functions in labour, which embrace both knowing and being. I cannot quote. It is not necessary. But here we reach slam bang up against one of those astonishing parallelisms which show the inherent dialectic in human society. Hegel had followed his system to the end and established the faculty of thought (through his World-Spirit) as the moving principle of the Universe. Under this banner, he had linked being and knowing. And he had made thought *free*, creative, revolutionary (but only for a few philosophers). Marxism followed him and established human labour as the moving principle of human society. Under this banner, Marx linked being and knowing, and made labour and therefore thought, free, creative, revolutionary, for all mankind. Both in their ways abolished the contradiction between being and knowing. Now if the party is the knowing of the proletariat, then the coming of age of the proletariat means the abolition of the party. This is our new Universal, stated in our baldest and most abstract form.[15]

Basically, for James, out of workers' movements we will find new forms of political organization:

> I do not propose to spend more than ten lines on the "leninist concept of the party," that noose around our throats. For our one world, our socialized world, the party must be the organized labour movement. To believe that the party is less a vanguard party because it contains all the workers "to a man," that is today a completely reactionary concept and is in essence Trotskyism. It cannot be defended without leading step by step to the most reactionary concepts of the proletariat. A few minutes of reflection should show this. *The vanguard of the vanguard organizes itself as it*

always has, on the basis of a strenuous analysis of the objective movement of society.[16]

For James, the kind of party organization that must take place will grow out of the actual struggle. To return to the "Leninist party," let alone to make a Lacanian ontology of the split subject the basis of such a party, is to fail to heed dialectical thinking in the sense to which James gives it. In a profound sense, the call to return to the Party and with it the need for phallic leaders takes us to the very heart of what James is arguing in *Notes on Dialectics*: dialectical thinking never rests on static, theoretical truths but always changes as movements themselves demand that change. In the previous chapter, I quoted Rosa Luxemburg's critique of the dictatorship of the proletariat, even as defined by Lenin. For Luxemburg, this is precisely because the ideal of socialism did not simply rest on Lenin's formulation of what and how the Paris Commune had taught us about the dictatorship of the proletariat. For Luxemburg, we would need in socialism, prior to the transition to communism, the most radical forms of participatory democracy because the move to undo the relationships of exploitation would have to involve as many voices as possible in order to begin to live together differently. In that way, Luxemburg herself moves to a different understanding of how the real socialist movement would need to produce a different way of being human together through radical democracy, which for her was the dictatorship of the proletariat. It is not that Luxemburg did not believe that certain forms of suppression of the capitalist class would be necessary, but she also argued strongly that those forms of suppression, even and especially when necessary, had to be submitted to constant challenges that would allow new relations of humanity to arise out of the barbarism that both James and Luxemburg saw as characterizing relations between human beings in the early twentieth century. In that sense, the stored-up wisdom that Luxemburg herself sought in her break with the Bolsheviks was crucial to her redefinition of the ideal of socialism away from the dictatorship of the proletariat to the form of socialism that would have a different content than the one to which Lenin gave it under the brutal necessities imposed by the concrete context in Russia. To be fair to Lenin, as James is, Lenin himself was very aware that the universal of socialism, even as he understood it as the workers' state, was unrealizable in Russia. And if he never lost sight of his own concept of the universal, which would lead us to communism, he also understood at the end of his life that it would be necessary to undo the corruption that he already saw growing in the Bolshevik Party. Luxemburg saw that such corruption was inevitable where there was too much centralism, but neither Luxemburg nor Lenin would have denied the need for a party. The question is rather about what kind and what relations to the movements on the ground so as not to fall behind what is most progressive and far-reaching—most revolutionary—in those movements. The recent attempts to make the psychoanalytic subject the basis of a so-called revolutionary understanding of the human, even what we could be and become in socialism, is not only Eurocentric but fails to take into account the central point exemplified by the life and thought of committed revolutionaries such as Lenin, Luxemburg, and James: *what it means to be human is always changing.* Is such dialectical thinking close to what I have called political spirituality? The answer is yes, and that is why James's work on Hegel is so important.

POLITICAL SPIRITUALITY AND JAMES'S RETHINKING OF DIALECTICAL MATERIALISM

What makes *Notes on Dialectics* so important to us is that its rethinking of dialectics completely rejects the idea that there is any *science* of dialectical materialism. To put it in James's own language, the way in which Essence operates is through the constant transformation, or negation, of prior identities—including the identities that would capture the ideals of the labor movement:

> The essence is the fact that something continually becomes something else and negates it because it isn't what the thing that is becoming wants to be. This "being" that it becomes, we know from the Doctrine of Being has "become" out of Nothing. All immediate being comes out of Nothing and can go back to nothing. The difference with Essence is that it creates a lot of different beings; they go back to nothing, but Essence keeps on trying, for poor Essence *is* the fact that he has to keep on trying. He is a kind of being that does not rest at becoming nothing but from his very nature must keep on trying and trying again.[17]

Indeed, throughout *Notes on Dialectics*, James uses Hegel's *Science of Logic* to analyze the labor movement itself as constantly shifting as the ideals postulated by the movement are transformed in the course of struggles, and as those ideals are enriched and changed, the labor movement becomes an experience that carries these transformations within itself. As we have already seen, James's own reading of Lenin is that *State and Revolution* articulated the Universal of what socialism could be, but as I also pointed out James believed that it was impossible to realize it in Russia. According to James, Lenin grasped the extent of this tragedy in his last writings, although he never backed away from positing the ideal of socialism as he had laid it out in *State and Revolution* in which every cook would govern. In his last article, "Better Fewer, But Better" (1923), Lenin faced the possibility that the creation of the peasant cooperatives was as good as he would ever get toward the ideal of socialism that he nevertheless continued to hold onto. "There is something infinitely pathetic and infinitely splendid," as James writes, "in the way Lenin, sick, watching the state running away, watching with his realistic vision the vast backwardness of Russia, still digs out of the harsh reality some programme, striving to realize the Universal. That is being a revolutionary."[18] As I discussed earlier, James's entire engagement with both Hegel and Lenin's own reading of Hegel is that, ultimately, we now need a transformed notion of socialism and the role of the Party within it.

I have two points I'm making here. The first is that following Hegel—and James's interpretation of Lenin's reading of Hegel—the ideal always grows out of confrontation with the real. Thus, it was the actual struggles of the workers themselves that led Lenin not only to *State and Revolution* but also to the recognition of the Soviets as a new form of workers' organization. But the second point is that even as he is struggling in 1923 with the corruption of the Party bureaucracy, Lenin understands that he must continue to postulate a universal—the universal, here, being the socialist program of workers' cooperatives, which he tried to describe and defend in his last article. Against the claims of certain Euro-American political theory in which theory is mainly engaged in "critique" as something separate from the struggle for political hegemony, the entire point of *Notes on Dialectics* is that what is called "theory" is actually the *embodiment of ideals in actual programs that grow out of the concrete struggle of people.* This is why James understood his own work as a revolutionary to postulate socialist ideals in the concrete form of a program, as he did in reference to the miners' struggles of the 1980s:

> Leninism *never* accepted the organizational limitations of the enemy. By methods which the bureaucracy would call "illegal" the *revolutionary* struggle against the bureaucracy must be carried on in the unions themselves. This alone would revolutionize the practice of the party. I shall now, by means of example only, make one or two excursions into the concrete. As a logical line for concretization, I propose for the miners:
>
> 1. They themselves, committees of miners, form the plan. They know better how to do it than anyone else.
>
> 2. They themselves, e.g., in Britain, visit American mines (and vice versa) in order to compare methods of work, machinery, etc.
>
> 3. They themselves who made the plan must be responsible for its being carried out.
>
> 4. They themselves will distribute the special allowances of food, clothing, allocate housing, distribute scarce goods in their neighbourhood.[19]

As we saw in chapter 2, James came to understand the way in which Black struggles in the United States postulate a different ideal and a different program consistent with the revolutionary significance of socialist struggles against racial capitalism. I am not, then, simply defending James's own attempt to lay out a specific program as one we should adopt now. Our point is deeper: the task of the revolutionary is to embody the ideals that grow out of the real (i.e., concrete struggles) but also that those ideals, in turn, change what the very nature of the real *is*. Ideals, when embodied in material reality, *change* the very nature of that reality: the "object" is changed through a constantly transformed consciousness. To remind us of the significance of how object becomes subject in dialectical materialism, I turn to Paget Henry's important engagement with *Notes on Dialectics*. In his excellent work on James's turn to Hegel's *Science of Logic*, Henry emphasizes the self-transformations inherent in James's own journey as a thinker and activist who is always moving beyond himself. James writes that in his early work he wrote through a ludic/poetic persona that produced such great works as his novel *Minty Allen*. But in the novel itself, the main character learns that his greatest teachers in the world that he is struggling to understand are not the elites in European universities but the people he engages with in the streets and daily encounters. With these encounters comes the brutal confrontation with colonial oppression. This confrontation turns him not only to activism but to a commitment to Trotskyism and the Socialist Workers' Party as the "way" to socialist revolution. His engagement with Trotskyism turned, once again, to a dilemma inherent in the elitism of the party that, far from unleashing the creative spontaneity of the workers, actually blocks it by reinstating a divide between *being* and *knowing* that Hegel's *Logic* will help him undo at the level of philosophy. Henry rightly describes James as a transcendental thinker, but in a specific sense. To quote Henry on the transcendental in Caribbean philosophy:

> By the transcendental dimensions of Caribbean philosophy I am referring to the regional history of practices of interrupting normal routines of disciplinary thought to examine, repair, or replace the *a priori* or the always already presupposed categoric foundations of the discipline or discourse that one is using. In turning his searchlight on these foundations, the key *a priori* categories and claims that James borrowed from Hegel were the subject/object relationship, the mutual determination of subject and object in any given knowing situation, the necessary dualities that were inherent in different subject/object relationships, and Hegel's claim that to grasp the full potential of the object of study, it should not be seen only as substance or material object but also as subject.[20]

The synthesis in James's own life led him into what Henry calls his embrace of "sociohistorical poetics" found in works such as *The Black Jacobins*. The certitudes of revolutionary righteousness had to once again be put into motion, breaking the tiresome capture of revolutionary creativity by party leaders in the abstract categories of the Understanding. As we have seen, he finds in Hegel the type of dialectical thinking that will allow him to do just that once Hegel has been "creolized." James rejects the final move of Hegel's *Logic* in which the self-reflexive dialectical motion of both subject and object completes itself in Divine Unity that can grasp itself as such in Absolute Knowledge. Again, to quote Henry:

> [W]hen we approach the object of knowledge as subject, it is precisely this categoric infrastructure of permanence that we must be able to dissolve

and surpass. Within the permanent formations of the Understanding we must be able to see the binary opposites that are in sharp conflict. Even more basic, we must be able to dissolve the Understanding's construction of the subject/object relationship and its correlated *a priori* categories of subject and object constitution. This transcendental work is going to be necessary for us to see what the object was before it reached this particular point in its formation and what it might be after it. However, to dissolve the "fixing" and other constitutive effects of the Understanding, we are going to need the aid of two epistemic capabilities: the first is that of a phenomenological suspension, which would enable us to interrupt or halt the "fixing" operations of the Understanding. The second is a self-reflective dialogical logic such as Hegel's. In other words, we are going to need a logic that can grasp the rise and fall, or the "draining out," of one subject/object relationship and the rise of another. It is important to stress here that this new logic must come with a change in the knowing subject as an integral part of a new knowing situation.[21]

Revolution in the flourishing of each and all of us as the collective subject of our own history is why this would be a completely new praxis of being human. Henry shows us how James ultimately reintegrated the ludic/poetic persona, producing such works as *Beyond a Boundary*. The struggle to reconcile the objectivity of the labor movement, and with it revolution, is also for Henry a profound subjective journey of constant struggle within himself. It sets us in motion and keeps us moving both through our own struggles to "know" who we are and, as participants in struggle, to be continuously open to new forms of struggle that emerge in the streets.

This is why Henry's own description of James's self-transformation is a central part of the argument in this chapter. Because Hegel's famous idea that substance becomes subject implicates us in how we are, and must be, engaged in a constant practice of self-transformation at the same time as we try to grasp any new objective reality that arises out of concrete struggle. Programs change and revolutionaries also change in their very grappling with the reality that revolutionary struggle is always transforming into something other than we took it to be. This is not, however, to be confused with the Trotskyite notion of "permanent revolution." For James, unlike the struggle for *socialism*, the reason Trotsky's conception of "revolution" is "permanent" is precisely because it is not connected to any kind of actual program: "Trotsky soared into the thin abstractions of the permanent revolution. *Nothing* came of it. Nothing. And it was Lenin's concrete theories, dealing with the actual, the Individual, from which came all the wonderful insights and illumination which enriched the notion of *socialism*."[22] Here we are returned to Rosa Luxemburg and her own critique of the Bolsheviks, for if new ideals are to be able to grow out of real struggles, those struggles must permit the widest forms of participatory democracy and the collective contestation of even the most cherished revolutionary ideals in the name of those ideals themselves. This means that the *new humanity* that both James and Luxemburg recognize as the universal that socialism proclaims to realize can never be captured by any ontology of the human being but can only be what Sylvia Wynter calls a collective *praxis of being human*, for those of us who have grown up in the context of racial capitalism can scarcely begin to imagine what any new species of humanity, to use Fanon's famous phrase, might look like.

For James, as for Luxemburg, this means the certitudes of theoretical righteousness must be put into motion, breaking the tiresome capture of revolutionary creativity by party leaders and intellectuals in the abstract categories of the Understanding. And as we have seen, James finds in Hegel the type of dialectical materialism that will allow him to do just that. James's creolization of dialectical materialism thus moves against what Hegel, in his critique of Kant, would call the "Understanding." Kant famously argued that the conditions of finite reason allow human beings to grasp the objective truth of scientific laws. But famously for Kant, the great ideals, which have always informed revolutionary struggles, cannot be grasped by the Understanding. The key to the *Critique of Pure Reason* is that ideals can never be reduced to an objective reality that can be definitively *known* through science. As James puts it, the Understanding imparts a fixed persistence to ideals that can never have such persistence. I agree with Kant that ideals are always *aesthetic* ideas that can be *configured* but never *known*. I need to be clear that by aesthetic ideas Kant did not mean the reduction of the ethical to the aesthetic; rather, he meant that these ideals could be subjected to judgement but not to *knowledge*. Ethical ideals can therefore always be contested and changed since they are about judgment—even when we seek consensus in such judgment, they are always contestable in that they involve a configuration not just of how the ideals are *imagined* but how they are *attempted* in new forms of institutionalization. Ultimately, Hegel would bring the ideal and the real together in Absolute

Knowledge, but Kant's point was to maintain the ideal as separate from science. Therefore, in a deep sense, revolutionaries are always thinking through the struggle and postulating ideals as they grow and develop out of actual struggles, otherwise they remain hopelessly abstract. But to configure these ideals, for James, means to risk embodying them in the development of a program. Such ideals, as Luxemburg would remind us, must also be open to constant challenge as it is only through radical participatory democracy that we could materially engage with others in a way that allows us to reimagine who and how we are in a world of relations beyond exploitation. I discussed earlier that, for James's interpretation of Lenin, the Party as the Knowing and the Being of the proletariat still had to remain separate, at least in terms of the struggle of the Russian Revolution. But with James and Luxemburg, we are confronted with how new forms of struggle can only arise when we challenge this very divide between Being and Knowing. (Of course, Luxemburg did not put it that way because, unlike James, she was not working with Hegel's *Science of Logic*.) What this means is that all forms of elitism that maintain a divide between Being and Knowing—including the divide between the poor masses who *are* and the so-called intellectuals who *know*—must be completely undone in revolutionary struggle. Here, then, we see how far away James's radical rethinking of dialectical materialism takes us from the "Diamat" of the Third International where Stalin falls prey to an Understanding in which the Party can announce the Truth of what is, in fact, never reducible to truth in any scientific sense. By turning dialectical materialism into a "science" and literally killing off those who disagreed with the official Truth, the struggle is captured by the kind of frozen dictatorship that can never be revolutionary. Indeed, this is why, for James, even Trotsky fell prey to the Understanding even as he tried to resist Stalin's scientificization of dialectical materialism. In the end, Trotsky was too far removed from the concrete struggle and the Fourth International could only react against Stalinism as the negation of everything that Lenin had fought for and dreamt of in *State and Revolution*. But for James, again following Hegel, the negation of the negation is always an affirmation of a *new ideal* embodied in concrete programs.

James may have rejected "Spirit" in Hegel's sense of the Absolute Idea that ultimately gives us knowledge of all that is in Absolute Knowledge, but I believe his rewriting of dialectical materialism and his lifetime of struggle with revolution—and, of course, James would point out that the two are inseparable—exemplify what I have called "political spirituality." It is the *spirit of revolution* to fight within concrete struggles, to postulate ideals, and to understand that even if we "understand" the ideal of socialism as imagining a new way of being human, the realization of that ideal must include all of us. In that sense, for James, the withering away of the state is also the withering away of the Party as something that governs us from outside our own collective struggles. Political spirituality is thus exactly the spirit of revolution James seeks to keep alive in his *Notes on Dialectics*. Spirit is no longer going to lead us to Absolute Knowledge or the German *Rechtsstaat*, as Hegel imagined. But it will enable us to begin, together, the reimagination and embodiment of new institutions, of new ways of living, of new ways of organizing the economy. And if we try to make those new realities out of the dream of a new humanity, then we will always be changing, arguing, and redeveloping those institutions that we have built so that we do not fall into the fiction of fixed persistence James associates with capture by the Understanding. The spirit of revolution is not an abstract "permanent revolution" as conceived by Trotsky. Rather, it proceeds through the concrete attempts at liberation and institutional innovation that we have seen throughout the Global South as people struggle to imagine what it might mean to decolonize our world, or in Black struggles that postulate a new way of being human beyond the brutalities of racial capitalism. As James teaches us, using Hegel's own concept of Experience, we learn and indeed take into ourselves and our movements the lessons from prior struggles—what Luxemburg famously called the "school of experience"—to revolutionize our world. This is why, as Paget Henry points out in his own work on James, *self-transformation* is integral to what I call political spirituality for we must change ourselves as our struggles demand of us nothing less than the constant reimagination and rebuilding of new ways of being human together in a socialist world—a world that, as both James and Fanon insist, would finally be the *beginning* of human history. These self-transformations are what Henry has called the "vertical dramas of consciousness" that must accompany any "horizontal" struggle for economic and political reorganization if we are to be able to even *imagine* what it might be like to live beyond capitalist exploitation, which is why, in *The Spirit of Revolution*, we situated our understanding of political spirituality precisely at the intersection of the horizontal and vertical revolutions.[23]

The "self-transformations" Henry reads in James's work, and which I place at the heart of political spirituality, should in no way be confused with individualism and especially neoliberal forms of "self-help." On the contrary, they bring us to the significance of *transindividuality* as part and parcel of any truly dialectical thinking of the world and our place in it. While there are some resources for thinking about transindividuality in European philosophy, including Spinoza, Simondon, and a certain reading of Hegel, I want to foreground the importance of African philosophy here, as it is only in African philosophy that transindividuality is fully grasped in all its ontological, ethical, and political richness. In the South African philosophy of *uBuntu*, for instance, every person is born into a web of affective relations that constitutes our world. But we are not reducible to this transindividual entwinement; rather, each person has a *responsibility* to materialize our singularity in our relations with others. The African practice of burying the umbilical cord, then, is not an empty ritual but sets the person on her path and shows that we only become ourselves once our mother has brought us into being through her labor and the support of the community. Ceremonies and rituals such as this materially teach us that we are never just "ourselves" but that we exist in an affective world in which all that we do affects all others. This is not what some Anglo-American philosophers would call a "consequentialist" notion such that ethics are determined by the "consequences" of our actions, as such, theories still presume external relations between autonomous individuals. In uBuntu, on the other hand, ethics is embedded in the very transindividual nature of being itself because any harm we might do to another human being reverberates and manifests itself as violence not only to whatever person(s) we might have harmed but to the community—and indeed the cosmos—as a whole. There is no way to extricate ourselves from our transindividual reality and no justification that could remove us from the affective connectivity that gives us the universe in which we live. This is not modern "liberalism" versus traditional "communitarianism" as it is often presented in tired Anglo-American debates where the "individual" is threatened by being subsumed in the "community." It is an understanding that as *individuating beings*—and not "individuals"— what we *are* depends on our relations with others. Such a dependence implies an ethical obligation both to the generations that have come before and those who are not yet here, as well as an understanding that your realization of your personhood is inseparable from ours. It is this transindividual reality that both allows capitalism to materialize an affective world in which our relations with others are exploitative and violent *and* that allows new forms of solidarity to arise again and again and transform who and what we are. For if we are all constituted within an affective web, then when joined in concrete struggle for a more just world, who and what we are is completely transformed by others, and this creativity that is unleashed through transindividuality is what gives spontaneous insurrectional activity its power to actually change our world. Unlike recent Euro-American turns to relational, affective, and entangled ontologies, uBuntu is therefore *inherently political* in that it demands that we struggle to bring the ontological fact of our transindividual being into being within a world of social relations where each person works toward the flourishing of others and of all. This is why uBuntu has been key to the South African struggle for decolonization and against apartheid and why it continues to be called upon today in the ongoing struggles to fulfill the socialist promise of the Freedom Charter.

Transindividuality is not a term that either James or Hegel uses, but it is at the heart of Hegel's *Science of Logic*, which in James's interpretation rewrites how materiality operates and manifests itself. By using Hegel's categories, James shows us a different way of opening the dialectic to help us grapple with our collective history of revolutionary struggle and, as I am arguing, implicit in that rereading of our collective revolutionary struggle is a notion of transindividuality that is perhaps best grasped through the resources of African philosophy such as uBuntu. This shifting of the geographies of reason within revolutionary thinking—both through James's "creolized" Hegel and through African thought—brings us back to epistemic humility inherent to political spirituality. Political spirituality is necessarily both humbling and demanding in that we must have the courage to face the limits of any of the actual attempts to realize a decolonized world in which the new humanity dreamt by socialism is concretized. There is no such thing as an absolute failure in such struggles, which perhaps takes us back to Lenin's haunting phrase "Better Fewer, But Better." When James tells us that the "Essence" of struggle always includes stored-up wisdom, he means that the lessons from past struggles have become part of what struggle *is* today: the very ideals that we are struggling to actualize now are themselves an archive of past struggles. But as James reminds us, revolutionaries must embody these ideals in a program. To make this more concrete, let us take the example of prison abolition. For example, FRELIMO, the revolutionary party for Mozambican liberation, abolished traditional prisons as crucial to decolonization. These prisons, which had been established by Portuguese colonization, were replaced by a complex system of community services in which retribution and punishment as ideals to justify imprisonment were replaced by accountability and responsibility. And this struggle to create innovative institutions demanded a reconfiguration of the ideals that guided the efforts at institutional decolonization in the first place. The complex history of FRELIMO is beyond the scope of this book, but for James, people's struggles for institutional innovation do not disappear into thin air—they go on to become integral to the very essence of revolutionary struggle. James's way of thinking about the essence of struggle, through a creolized and decolonized Hegel, pulls us beyond ourselves and beyond any sedimented ideals that become a "persistent finite" masquerading as the Infinite. This pull to the beyond is therefore part and parcel—indeed the spirit—of the struggle, not outside it. The spirit is infinite because it pulls us *beyond* our finite selves as we pursue the great ideals that guide us. The infinite here—which I would call the spirit of revolution—moves through each finite person, in each finite struggle, only if we endure the changes demanded of us and only if we are fearless enough to attempt to create a world in which justice, dignity, and freedom are something more than a mockery of those ideals themselves.

PRACTICAL CONSIDERATIONS FOR REVOLUTIONARY SOCIALISM IN THE CARIBBEAN NEW LEFT

I have focused in the last section of this chapter on the significance of James's own turn toward Hegel, as it returns us to the centrality of "spirit" as self-transformation and is at the very heart of socialist struggles. This focus is on what Paget Henry himself has called the "vertical revolution," the revolution within each one of us as we try to project an existential self who is capable of not only fighting in a new world but of living in it. I will return to Paget Henry's conception on the difference between the horizontal and the vertical revolution shortly, but before doing so, we need to examine James's inspirational force on the actual organizational efforts in the Caribbean New Left in the 1960s and 1970s.

Generations were inspired by C. L. R. James's vision and program of insurrectional struggles from the ground up as the basis for a socialist society rooted in cooperatives in production and councils in all levels of government run by the worker themselves. I will explore two of those movements shortly: New Beginnings in Trinidad and the Caribbean Liberation Movement in Antigua. But before doing so, I need to discuss that James himself moved away from his own position in *Notes on Dialectics* that the age of the party had run its course. Indeed, in James's works *Facing Reality* and *The Advancing Socialist Society*, two books that celebrated the rebellion in Hungary in 1956 and other insurgencies, he made a distinction between modern industrial societies with an organized proletariat and the struggle of colonized peoples to free themselves from the chains of colonization. In such struggles, a party would be necessary. He returns to something like this position in *Party Politics in the West Indies*. I say "something like" because his emphasis is on a kind of "liberation Leninism," where the party facilitates forms of organization that need to be in place before the struggle for socialism, and with it the realization of the program he advocated for in *Notes* as well as in many other texts.

In his discussion on Lenin and the trade unions with Franklin Harvey and Alfie Roberts, they both push James very hard on the necessity of the trade unions in the struggle for socialism.

> Roberts: But to get back to something. I don't believe this is the impression you really want to give or impart: that trade unions have to be the prerequisite for any meaningful socialist construction?
>
> James: Not the trade unions, but the proletariat, the organized proletariat.
>
> Harvey: They must be organized in some sort of movement. It is not bound to be a union.

James: No, it must be a union. What is the strength of the Oilfield Workers Trade Union? They are united, disciplined, and organized by the very mechanism of capitalist production. That is the strength of the Oilfield Workers Trade Union. They are not organized by Weekes and union organizers. It is the fact that they are working in a large industry, coming to work every morning, and working together. That is the basis of organization. And that is what Marxism means.[24]

They both reject the idea that socialism, as James himself has understood it, is now impossible in the Caribbean. Both Roberts and Harvey reject James's position, and yet James himself remains true to the spirit of his anti-elitism and his faith in the workers: "We used to put it forward. I lectured to the Oil Field Workers Trade Union and I said to the workers 'we cannot create any socialism here.' There is nothing that I wouldn't tell a worker."[25]

The debate with James was not over his vision of what constituted socialism, nor was it over his understanding that socialism had a self-transformative dimension. James was unwavering in his commitment to socialism as the self-organization of the workers in production and government, and with that leadership a whole new understanding of what it meant to govern. All the fundamental definitions of life would change as socialism challenged all the hierarchies that define human beings under capitalism. This sweeping challenge is what I have discussed as the significance of James's turn to Hegel to understand the existential dimensions of what socialism would demand in all of us, what we will return to again as Paget Henry's vertical revolution. A laborer who cooperatively managed a factory would no longer be a laborer, both in reality and self-projection. The debate with James was whether socialism, in his understanding, could be realized in the Caribbean without what James saw as an organized proletariat. Hence his emphasis on the trade unions and a party that could facilitate that organization: "liberation Leninism." However, both Harvey and Roberts were important leaders of the Caribbean New Left which rejected James's skepticism and sought to realize socialism in the Caribbean, though they were only two of many voices that remained faithful to view of socialism as James understood it. I turn now to two of the most important movements of the Caribbean New Left.

THE NEW BEGINNING MOVEMENT IN TRINIDAD

The New Beginning Movement (NBM) in part grew out of the activists that organized around the *Vanguard* newspaper of the Oil Field Workers Trade Union. However, it moved beyond economic trade union issues to become a voice for the Jamesian program of direct democracy through the creation of cooperatives throughout industry and other forms of self-organization in government. James did not believe that the struggle for his own program of self-emancipation of the oppressed was possible in the Caribbean of his time, as I discussed above. It is beyond the scope of this book to do anything like a rich history of the movements in the Caribbean New Left, but that said, they offered highly original programs for a transition to socialism that insisted on fidelity to James's program in *Notes*. As we already saw, Harvey rejected any return to party politics, which James seemed to think was the only real option in the Caribbean given the weakness of the organized proletariat. In his *Rise and Fall of Party Politics in Trinidad and Tobago*, Harvey went so far as to argue that such a party could only be a means of social oppression of the creative empowerment of people's new forms of social organization.[26]

Simply put, the organization of a party, even a mass party, would not be a new beginning, but rather the reinforcement of bureaucratic power that would undermine any transitional program with explicit socialist aspirations. The NBM did have such a program. To quote Matthew Quest, who is one of the most significant historians of the Caribbean New Left:

> In a statement "What We Want Now—Class Struggle for Power" NBM offered a type of transitional program. They called for unconditional lifting of the state of emergency, the immediate release of all political prisoners the lift of the bans on demonstrations in Port of Spain and San Fernand, and on books, magazines, and other radical literature. NBM insisted freedom of assembly without police intimidation and a call for the repeal of the ISA was mandatory. They advocated establishment of "labor tribunals" which were to consist of "60% of elected workers representatives, 30% employers' representatives, and 10% peoples' government representatives."

Labor laws establishing a minimum wage and rejecting compulsory overtime, and the taking over of agricultural estates and idle lands and redistributing the land among everyday farmers was suggested. NBM argued all new laws, social services, community improvement projects, and initiatives should be forged at the community level through elected village councils and assemblies. Creating jobs that target the development of Nariva, Oropouche, and Caroni swamps could solve unemployment.

Demanding unconditional resignation of the government, including all officers of the police, military, coast guard and all members of the judiciary; a vision of an alternative form of government by popular committees distinguished by the capacity of instant recall of all representatives surfaced. A provisional assembly shall create a new constitution that ordinary people shall approve. NBM implored the people of Trinidad to "bring your own government into being."[27]

Clearly this program was indebted to James's vision of how socialism could move beyond any party form.

James famously idealized Athenian democracy as one that could be the basis of a memory of future possibility in *Every Cook Can Govern*. Of course, that history was "enchanted," but James's telling of Athenian democracy held a promise that the very idea that every cook could govern was not a hopeless utopian fantasy. The NBM, on the other hand, turned instead to East Indian and African practices of communal self-organization as crucial to the struggle against the cultural contempt of colonization. Again, to quote Matthew Quest,

> While NBM noted the traditional idea of governance in India before British colonialism was patriarchal, and based on the male lineage of the family leading heads of households, communities "formed the panchayat whose chairman became the 'father' of the village." These village councils sent delegates to provincial coordinating bodies deciding on all questions of taxation and economic planning.
>
> When the panchayat deliberated, the guardian leadership made most decisions but "all who wanted could attend and could have their say." The panchayat handled all judicial and economic decisions but had no legal authority merely a moral authority. This moral authority seldom disobeyed, society gained its spiritual strength from this institution.

NBM responded to the contention that panchayat was not a democratic institution reminding the leaders emerged from and lived among the ordinary villagers. The village rulers were "of the people, and not above or apart from them." This closeness of leadership to ranks prevented unethical behavior. Where immoral leaders were uncovered, they were exposed and forced to live within the village and face ostracism as the penalty for corruption.[28]

The NBM also turned to this history of African communal practices. This history was inspired by modern experimental reinterpretations of Julius Nyerere's *Ujamaa Socialism* and Ron Karenga's *Nguzo Saba*, which gave modern meaning to precolonial life. The emphasis was on community engagement in which anyone could speak, even if African chiefs had control over land. No one denied that these structures were patriarchal and set in precolonial history, but there was a different philosophy of how we could be together. The point was not that these communal forms of engagement were enough to be implemented again. This debate continues in contemporary comparative African philosophy around the Zulu word *uBuntu* and the Woolof word *Nite*.[29]

Yes, there is a very different philosophical understanding of what it means to be human as we live in an affective chain in which we can only flourish through the support of others. Is there something "African" in these philosophies? Humanity is a collective achievement; one we must practice together in order to challenge the brutal reality of racialized capitalism. That these philosophies are African is not made up, nor are these philosophies and the organizational promise they bring with them something that is just there to awaken and put in place. Instead, like all philosophies, this is a philosophy that is constructed and always toward the future.[30] What *uBuntu* and *Nite* would mean now in struggle against racialized capitalism is something to be continuously reinterpreted and reimagined. The NBM did not go into how we are to rethink African philosophy, and indeed history, to recognize that there are African ways of being human that have something to teach us now. But the underlying lesson was similar in that these forms of organization could point us to a different future. There is no pure precolonial philosophy or forms of social organization to which we can return, but the presentation of a different history rooted in African heritage is one that could be mobilized. The ultimate reactionary thinking is that everything is what it is and that is that, but James turned to Hegel because nothing is what it is but is always in motion, changing. Of course, these histories are "enchanted," but that enchantment has a purpose, not the least because they work against the cultural contempt for the colonized.[31]

TIM HECTOR AND THE ANTIGUA CARIBBEAN LIBERATION MOVEMENT

On his return to Antigua in 1967, Tim Hector developed a sweeping institutional plan to realize the kind of people's power that was called for by James. Key to the realization of the program was the creation of people's councils. Hector was critical of VC Bird's attempt to realize Black democratic socialism primarily through nationalization of the sugar plantations. Ultimately the economic crisis that seemed unsolvable under VC Bird's nationalization strategy led Hector to move toward a form of state capitalism that centered on the economic boost provided by the promotion of tourism.[32] For Hector, the challenge of socialism went way beyond the question of ownership, state or private. People's power, including Black power, had to become fully realized and worked out in an entirely cooperative form of governance in both industry and politics. To quote Hector,

> Socialism isn't not nationalization. Socialism is not a vanguard party in power. Socialism is not the commanding heights of the economy brought under state control. Socialism is not state decrees. Socialism is not "Benefits" for the masses. Socialism is the independent creative spirit of the mass of the population given the room and the opportunity to create new institutions at work, for the re-organization of production in the interest of the majority of the toilers and so creating popular democratic organs of self-management in society and therefore a new culture.[33]

Like the NBM, Hector rejected any return to the vanguard party as necessary to politics in a former colony facing the difficulties of underdevelopment.[34] Indeed, he went one step further than NBM in laying a full-blown program of what socialism as the realization of people's power would mean now. Parliamentary representation would no longer be the primary means of governance, if it were to continue to exist at all. Instead, people would be organized into local councils. These councils would function as watchdogs to call out corruption and incompetence of elected representatives. In other words, elected representatives would be beholden to the councils. Of course, the question remained as to whether an organized system of councils would ultimately replace parliamentary government. How these councils would be formed was also debated. Would they be elected, created by lottery, or formed by some kind of system of volunteering? If every cook can govern, then the access to being an actual member of a council should be open to as many as possible. In terms of the economy, there would be three sectors: the National, the Industrial, and the Agricultural. Since the Antigua Caribbean Liberation Movement (ACLM) was not a vanguard party, it would not appoint the officials in the councils. Its role would be to facilitate and support these councils because ACLM activists were working from within the councils. They were not creating plans from outside and having party officials tell those involved how to implement the party's central plan. To quote Henry's description of the ACLM's people's power program,

> The economic dimensions of the black co-operative alternative were refashioned along similar lines. The earlier three-sector model remained the core of Hector's economy. This was going to be a national economy, but not one in which huge government bureaucracies controlled everything. Rather, it was going to be a national economy in which there would be "the direct voice of the people in the organization and development of every major enterprise that is the property of the nation." At the center of this popular involvement in the economy must be the working class, as dominant agent and major entrepreneur.
>
> In the state sector there would be a planning committee, "made up of technicians, workers and farmers." However, this was definitely not going to be a centrally planned economy. The goal of this planning was to launch and coordinate the transition from the neo-colonial/tourist economy to the new national economy, and how this state sector would relate concretely to the private and co-operative sectors. However, in both the co-operative and state sectors, assemblies or popular council models of governance would be introduced. For example, "ACLM will organize large co-operatives on government agricultural land, with state farms in each zone to give support and technical guidance to each co-operative." To further support these co-operatives, an Agricultural and Savings Bank would also be established, as well as a co-operatively run marketing company.[35]

As Henry further explains,

> Thus workers and farmers, through assemblies, would be in charge of significant areas of production, making key decisions, regarding output, wages, benefits, unemployment, the distribution of the surplus and its investment. Indeed these were the councils or assemblies that would in most cases also have the power to recall poorly performing political representatives from state offices. Thus Hector's critique of Libya's experiment with direct democracy was that its assemblies were "not based on production, but on residence." For Hector, socialism was the unity of working people organized in associations of co-operative producers, which clearly established the control of workers over both politics and economics.[36]

Hector's detailed development of what socialism demanded was not only visionary but practical. He never gave up on this sweeping transformation of every aspect of governance and production, but he did have to back off the timeline, though never as completely as James himself. The mass party would engage in preparations awaiting the next insurgency of the oppressed by participating in experiments in direct democracy. As Henry tells us, the ACLM was weakened not only internally but through major world events—notably the collapse of the Soviet Union but also the socialist struggles that ultimately lost power in Africa, South America, and the Caribbean. How and why their great experimental programs in socialism faltered and collapsed is beyond the scope of this book, in part because each deserves careful attention and analysis. But, of course, given the global nature of capitalism, the so-called waning of these experiments led movements like ACLM and NBM to lose their local force, and being called "unrealistic."[37]

A RETURN TO HENRY'S VERTICAL REVOLUTION AND POLITICAL SPIRITUALITY

The vast majority of this chapter has focused on James's turn to Hegel and the relevance of Hegel's notion of spirituality as infinite motion in material reality, which frames James's own process of self-transformation and his reconsideration of the role of the party in socialist politics. We may seem to have strayed from the emphasis on James's *Notes on Dialectics* to discuss the extraordinary movements of the Caribbean New Left, but I want to suggest that we have not. In Matthew Quest's excellent article on Tim Hector and Kwayana, Quest emphasizes that, for Hector and Kwayana,

> socialism was not simply a labor-theoretic economic discourse but was an *imaginary*, a means for cultivating alternative institutions and for designing a new society. The content of socialism for both Hector and Kwayana was a struggle of social classes but never a narrow political economy. Instead socialism was a civilization-ethic where the masses discover their own unfolding capacities.[38]

A civilization ethic understood as socialism returns us to political spirituality and Paget Henry's vertical revolution in two senses. Henry always emphasized that there is a horizontal as well as a vertical aspect to revolutionary transformation into a socialist society. We seem, in this last section, to have been focusing almost exclusively on the horizontal version, but what Henry has shown us is that the two are never and can never be separate, and this is what makes the legacy of the New Left in the Caribbean so important. The horizontal aspect of the revolution was a complete reorganization of society to implement the people's power. The vertical dimension was how we would have to transform ourselves existentially to begin to fight for such a society let alone to live in it. Neither the ACLM nor NBM emphasized Hegel, but the far-reaching works of these thinkers and their attempt to show us as concretely as possible about how we can live ethically together are infused with what Henry emphasizes as the vertical revolution.

The two aspects are as follows: how empowerment actually changes the very definitions of such commonplace notions as labor, ownership, hierarchy, and how we live within those as they have entrapped us. The second is how we need to project ourselves differently in order to live free of those entrapments and project ourselves differently as human beings who live together to control and structure our own societies. And, yes, now I would put that on a global plane. But there is a third aspect of the vertical revolution and what I call political spirituality that I want to emphasize, and that is humility. There are no geniuses who are going to tell us how and what to do—no Mao, no Stalin, let alone Bob Avakian—who are going to order us into the new communism. This is a profound lesson of the Caribbean New Left. There are no really "smart guys" who are going to tell us what to do and how communism is and how we have to realize it. They need to be left behind. In a lecture, the revolutionary and then constitutional court justice Albe Sachs asked us if we are still waiting for the beautiful people to arrive so there finally can be a world rooted in justice rather than the brutal exploitation of racialized capitalism.[39] He leaves us with a message crucial to political spirituality: the beautiful people are not coming. They are here, and they are us.

Chapter 4

Future Struggles
Stardust People and Democratic Socialism

We ended chapter 3 with a discussion of the great Caribbean experiments that not only embraced socialism as a "civilization ethic" but demanded that we not only think of new ways of democratically controlling all aspects of life together but sought and developed new forms of organization to realize a transformed humanity. Implicit in the idea of socialism as a "civilization ethic" is that socialism is not only a completely transformed economy but a new way of being human together. We would transform ourselves away from the relations of exploitation which dominate under capitalism. There is then both a vertical and horizontal aspect to revolution as Paget Henry continuously reminds us. We will turn to Henry's discussion of creole metaphysics shortly. For now, I want to emphasize that what a world worthy of stardust people (to use the term from Patrisse Khan-Cullors and Asha Bandele) demands is that we challenge all forms of sexual and erotic repression, and with it of course the opening of new forms of being together in personal as well as political relationships.

In the moving opening to the Black Lives Matter memoir, *When They Call You a Terrorist*, Patrisse Khan-Cullors and Asha Bandele describe the impact of a lecture by the astrophysicist Neil deGrasse Tyson that we are not only on the universe, we are also of it. We are made up of atoms and molecules that are traceable to the crucibles in the centers of stars that once exploded into gas clouds, and thus we are made of stardust. For Khan-Cullors, the significance of this realization is not only radically egalitarian but also has a magic to it that she finds in all the people close to her, whose stories she tells, that ultimately calls her to activism, to fight for the freedom, and to be one of the founders of a movement that has shaken our world, Black Lives Matter.[1]

In the 1990s, I advocated the notion of ethical feminism[2] to expand the reach of feminist struggles beyond those of women's freedom and equality, as important as those struggles are. Ethical feminism fought as feminists against oppressions that threw anyone beneath the bar of humanity. To deny the humanity of anyone was then a feminist issue. Therefore, ethical feminism was implicitly anti-racist, anti-imperialist, anti-war, and anti-capitalist, with a challenge to the liberal feminism that remained within the capitalist language of individualism and choice. The difference was put into practice. After 9/11, the liberal feminists celebrated women's rights in Afghanistan to not wear head scarves. None of us denied the oppressiveness of the Taliban, but an unjust war in the name of a freedom that explicitly targeted Islamic women? No way. With a comrade and long-time feminist leader Ann Snitow, we argued that the feminist solution was to support the Revolutionary Association of Afghan Women (RAWA) to at least be on the ballot in Afghanistan, an open vote that never happened. These women, and yes it was women-led, were true revolutionaries. They were the ones who ran the underground gynecology clinics and the hidden schools for girls. They also had a government in exile. Liberal feminists labeled them Maoists terrorists. They were of course against the unjust invasion of Afghanistan, a war that cost so many lives and ended with the Taliban in power. And so were those who supported RAWA. Out of the meetings and fundraisers an organization grew: Take Back the Future. We joined all the anti-war demonstrations, both against the invasions of Afghanistan and Iraq. But at home we also protested the targeting of the Islamic men who, even with green cards, had to be interrogated for possible terrorist activities. We marched at the request of African American mothers whose sons with minor mishaps were being given the choice of prison or to join the army. We did so as feminists and with the recognition that these were feminist issues even if, in both cases, they mainly target men. I remain very proud of the work of Take Back the Future, and I am deeply honored to have worked so closely with Ann Snitow who was such an important leader of the feminist movement in New

York City, for so many years always seeking innovative solutions to complicated often ferocious disagreements between feminists.

But I felt that, although almost all of us in Take Back the Future were socialists, I had not thought through enough the philosophical or activist groundings of ethical feminism. What was the connection of the vertical and horizontal aspects of democratic socialism? How can we rethink socialism as a "civilization ethic" that demands nothing less than how we must transform, think, and live together? I had immersed myself in European philosophy, but I found myself dissatisfied with the philosophical resources I found there. The Caribbean Philosophical Association (CPA) was founded around the same time as the uBuntu Project. The CPA called for the shifting of the geographies of reason. This shift sounded right to me as part of the process of decolonization but also helped me to find new ways of thinking about key concepts that allowed me to explore much more deeply both the theoretical and practical aspects of what I had called ethical feminism.

UBUNTU FEMINISM

The uBuntu Project began in 2003 with a small stipend from the Stellenbosch Institute for Advanced Study in South Africa. At first there was a great deal of skepticism on the part of mainstream white academics about whether uBuntu was actually a value that still held a substantial amount of purchase in the majority Black population. As a result, the project began with a series of interviews, the feedback from which, the interviewers anticipated, would shed some light on the question of whether or not that skepticism was justified. In short summation, the skepticism often turned on misconceived notions, which not only argued that uBuntu is premodern but also that it endorsed old-fashioned hierarchies such as patriarchy. It appeared that these skeptics worried about the very content of uBuntu—but they were not the only kind of skeptics. Other skeptics held that even if uBuntu had once been a powerful value important to the struggle for change in South Africa, it no longer played a major role among young people in the country. Indeed, it was challenged that many of the rituals were no longer practiced among young, urban, Black South Africans. In response to this skepticism, I joined with five young residents of Khayamandi, a township outside of Stellenbosch, to conduct interviews and discuss whether or not this skepticism was at all justified.

The five interviewers were all lifelong residents of Khayamandi and were deeply connected to the community. What the interviews ultimately showed was that the value of uBuntu remained extremely important; young Black South Africans still take the rituals seriously and practice them as a way of thinking about our fundamental interconnectedness, as well as a way of living it. The interviews also confirmed that uBuntu was considered to be at the heart of the way the community thought human beings should live their lives. Indeed, uBuntu was conceived by the interviewees as an African principle encapsulating what it means to be human and how all of social relationships are necessarily embedded in an ethical entanglement that begins at birth. These interviews provided helpful sociological insight showing that there was little basis for the skepticism the authors were initially met with; therefore, the importance of uBuntu needed to be promoted among all aspects of academic life, not undermined. But, as mentioned above, another one of the objections was that uBuntu was both premodern, as well as patriarchal in the worst sense of the word, as insisting on the authority of men over women. As Justice Ngcobo of the South African Constitutional Court has argued,[3] there was a time when most Africans were hunters and gatherers. At least hypothetically, during this time, an African notion of gender trusteeship developed. Under this ideal of trusteeship, women were entitled to certain kinds of care from men, but this kind of trusteeship, for Ngcobo, only made sense in those types of societies. But the question must be asked, can uBuntu push toward a more egalitarian modality of social relations and away from trusteeship? And, is this what is happening in South Africa now?

As time progressed, the uBuntu Project became involved in a number of on-the-ground issues that shifted the emphasis from interviews toward activism. From early on, the idea of an uBuntu Women's Center was raised. One idea that came out of the meetings was that a collective economic empowerment project should be established, which would offer employment to unemployed women in the township. The idea of a sewing collective was decided on, and with the assistance of a sangoma (a spiritual leader with whom I worked as an assistant), the project received sewing machines and other supplies. The idea was that unemployed women would sew "traditional clothing" that they could sell at an on-the-street marketplace. The sewing collective ran for about a year, and some of the women involved were able to earn desperately needed income for both themselves and their families. All profits were shared collectively in line with the principle of uBuntu. The deep sense of collectivity, borne out by the successes of the collective, was used to channel more enthusiasm toward the idea of an uBuntu Women's Center.

The initial interviews and the engagement with members of the Khayamandi community left me with the conviction that to regard uBuntu as either conservative or fundamentally patriarchal misunderstands its transformative potential. This is not to deny, however, that uBuntu has been deployed for conservative purposes. It is not something that can simply be uncovered. Like all values that claim roots in an indigenous past, that past is also grasped through recollective imagination and the struggle for a better future. This is certainly true in the case of what will later be discussed as revolutionary uBuntu.

The Philosophy of uBuntu

First of all, uBuntu cannot be reduced either to ontology, epistemology, or an ethical value system; that is, if one even wanted to speak in this regard in the terms of European philosophy. In a sense, uBuntu is all three. That uBuntu can be thought to be inclusive of all three demonstrates how major distinctions in European and Anglo-American philosophy are not replicated in African philosophy more generally. This already indicates how some of the major distinctions in the Anglo and European philosophical traditions are not reducible to European thinking and are not replicated entirely in African philosophy.

uBuntu is a philosophy on how human beings are intertwined in a world of ethical relations from the moment they are born. Fundamentally, this inscription is part of our finitude. We are born into a language, a kinship group, a tribe, a nation, and a family. We come into a world obligated to others, and those others are obligated to us. We are mutually obligated to support each other on our respective paths to becoming unique and singular persons. In European writing, the philosopher Benedict de Spinoza has often been linked to the idea of *transindividuality*.[4] Indeed, he is seen as one of the only thinkers to underscore transindividuality.[5]

This could be related to what D. A. Masolo[6] has called "participatory difference." For Masolo, participatory difference recognizes that each one of us is indeed different from all other people. The crucial part of this difference, however, is that we are also called to make a difference by contributing to the creation and sustenance of a human and ethical community. Critics of uBuntu, including those who conflate uBuntu with outdated modes of social cohesion and hierarchies, make the mistake of reducing uBuntu to an ethical ontology of a purportedly shared world. What is missed in the conservative critique is precisely the activism inherent in making a difference. In this manner, uBuntu clearly has an ideal edge. There is no end to the struggle to bring about a human world and to become an individual person who makes a difference within it. The acclaimed South African philosopher Mabogo P. More brings together different aspects of uBuntu in his profound yet succinct definition:

> In one sense, uBuntu is a philosophical concept forming the basis of relationships, especially ethical behavior. In another sense, it is a traditional politico-ideological concept referring to sociopolitical action. As a moral or ethical concept, it is a point of view according to which moral practices are founded exclusively on consideration and enhancement of human well-being; a preoccupation with the "human." It enjoins that what is morally good is that what brings dignity, respect, contentment, and prosperity to others, self, and the community at large. UBuntu is a demand for a respect for persons no matter what their circumstances may be. . . . In its politico-ideological sense it is a principle for all forms of social or political relationships. It enjoins peace and social harmony by encouraging the practice of sharing in all forms of communal existence.[7]

As an ethical as well as a politico-ideological concept, and one that encompasses categories that are often called ontology and epistemology, uBuntu always entails a social bond. But, one that is always in the course of being shaped and reshaped by the heavy ethical demands it puts on all its participants. And, why ontology and epistemology? As an ontology, uBuntu narrates how human beings are actually intertwined. It is therefore about the being of the human. But, the being of the human also constitutes how we see the world; for this intertwinement is inherently ethical. When we see or grasp the world, we epistemologically understand it through an inherent ethicality that inheres in our human being with inescapable obligations. Furthermore, since it is an ethical one, this social bond is always demanding the rethinking of what the ethical, and, therefore, what the politico-ideological demand. uBuntu in this sense encapsulates how we know the world, as well as how we are in it through the moral obligations as human beings who must live together. It implies the moralization of all social relations. And, this moralization of social relations is the one aspect of uBuntu that is unchanging.

The Concept of Governmentality under uBuntu

In European philosophy, most conceptions of social belonging are either rooted in fear or utility. In Thomas Hobbes, it was primarily fear that would lead individuals to relinquish their natural freedom and subordinate themselves to a Leviathan that would protect them from others who would constantly be a threat if there was no law to rule over them. In Kant, by contrast, the contract is inherently moral. And, in a deep sense, there are no individuals in Kant that are self determining. The social contract is hypothetical in so far as it imagines what moral individuals, who subordinated themselves to the moral law, might agree to. Kant's moral person is not an individual in the Hobbesian or utilitarian sense, but even if the social contract is hypothetical in that it entails that we project ourselves as moral human beings subordinated to the moral law in the Kingdom of Ends, as if we were already living together in the Kingdom, we can still conceive of social belonging through the social contract. Even though this will be a conception of the social contract that is substantially different from what the Hobbesian one is based on, it is still a conception of the social contract. For uBuntu, the very notion of the social contract misses the idea that human beings are born into an affective network that is constantly being transformed by the participants themselves. The idea, then, of social belonging is one in which the purpose of coming together under the law—or even, say, under the living customary law, the law of the majority of the Black population— would always demand that the purpose of any kind of government is to create a world in common and to enhance the publicly shared good. It would not be built out of fear or neutral exchanges in the free marketplace, or even the aesthetic idea of the Kingdom of Ends wherein we would together be acting morally to bring about a just world. It is both more active than that and the purpose is fundamentally different. Thus, uBuntu rejects the pessimistic ideas of human nature that pervade so much of European and Anglo and American political theory. Instead, it defends itself as a new way of being human together.

We need to judge uBuntu not simply because it is African or South African but, rather, because the philosophical project it offers is one of solidarity building. And, indeed, if one takes revolutionary uBuntu seriously as a project of "radical transformation," solidarity must be at the core. The phrase "revolutionary uBuntu" was coined by the Shack Dwellers movement, as well as other movements of the poor in South Africa, who argue that uBuntu itself is an anti-capitalist ideal and that neoliberal capitalism cannot be conceived as consistent with it. Economist Solomon Terreblanche, in his groundbreaking book *A History of Inequality in South Africa*, describes 354 years of patterns of unfree Black labor to underscore that the transformation in the country cannot move forward unless it completely undoes that history. For Terreblanche, the transformation of South Africa can only take place if the destructive aspects of this long history of unfree Black labor, which clearly began long before the institutionalization of apartheid, is completely reversed. This can only happen if some form of either social democracy or democratic socialism is implemented at the institutional level. But we can also read unfree Black labor as implying a telos that points toward a different history of free human beings living together under uBuntu. It is important to note that the phrase "unfree Black labor" unites both a race and a class; and in addition, it points to how the so-called modern project of neoliberal capitalism turns on forms of indentured servitude, which allow for the super exploitation of the large majority of humanity. Within South Africa, Terreblanche's powerful argument is that residues of unfree Black labor have completely undermined the transformation of the country. Two points need to be underscored here. First, that uBuntu points toward a conception of what it means to be a free human being who maintains that the human being must be unchained from unfree Black labor. And, second, there can be no serious transformation of South Africa without thoroughgoing economic transformation. In his book *Lost in Transformation*, Terreblanche pointedly argues that transformation has faltered or indeed failed because of the neoliberal economic policy of the African National Congress. It failed before what revolutionary uBuntu demands, namely, free individuals living and shaping their future as one that is always open to transformation.⁸

But there is another aspect of uBuntu important in this regard: uBuntu necessarily implies the struggle against anti-Black racism. Many figures in the history of African philosophy, from Frantz Fanon (1963) to Mabogo P. More (2005) to Lewis Gordon (2006) and many others have all argued that the struggle against racism is not only political and ethical but also philosophical. As stated before, it is philosophical because uBuntu challenges some of the primary distinctions made in Europe and Anglo-American philosophy such as ontology, epistemology, and ethics. But, it does so through the elaboration and narration of a new vision of humanism. To consider uBuntu seriously as a philosophy means to challenge racism. Indeed, it is to challenge the racism that inheres in the critique of racism too vague to have any moral, ethical, or political purchase. The uBuntu Project, as already indicated, has in a deep sense been both descriptive and prescriptive because the African ideal such as uBuntu could be universalized. To even hypothesize the reach of an African ideal in this manner implies an anti-racist stance that is not neutral, as if such neutrality could ever actually exist in research.

uBuntu and Current Debates in Euro-United States Feminism

Famously, in the United States, a debate broke out between feminists who argued for an ideal of justice and other feminists who, after the publication of *In a Different Voice*,⁹ by Carol Gilligan, advocated for the ethics of care. In short summation, the debate went something like this. Feminists who argued for justice as the overarching framework for feminist theory often held on to the notion of the "autonomous individual" and posited that women have been denied their autonomy. This denial of autonomy was a major ethical and political problem. Even the great thinker Simone de Beauvoir¹⁰ argued that the most important goal for women was to overcome the burden of their femininity and to live authentic and free lives, in the existential sense. The ways of thinking associated with femininity, for de Beauvoir, were bogged down by the imposition of gender stereotypes that functioned powerfully to prevent women from claiming their existential freedom. In short, it is no secret that de Beauvoir's work influenced generations of feminism, sometimes implicitly and sometimes explicitly so. For de Beauvoir, feminism began with breaking down or rejecting all the stereotypical lifestyles of the so-called good woman. First and foremost, women should reject marriage, and de Beauvoir particularly attacked the notion of motherhood. With the rejection of all these traditional and so-called feminine lifestyles, new ways of being a free human being unburdened by abject femininity could begin to arise. To embrace being a woman, for de Beauvoir—that is, to embrace sexual difference—was to be captured by these myths and stereotypes so forcefully imposed on women. Although many feminists, who saw justice as the ideal to be attained by women in the late 1960s and early 1970s, were not "de Beauvoirians," existentially speaking, their claim was that men and women were equal in their capacity to live autonomous lives.

According to Gilligan, thinkers like Lawrence Kohlberg argued that human beings went through stages of moral reasoning. The highest form of moral reasoning for Kohlberg, a type of moral reasoning that he and others associated with Kantian rationality, is the ability to actively abstract things from circumstances of context, and subsequently posit them as universally justifiable moral judgments. Kant himself, and perhaps Kohlberg as well, might reach that stage. But in Kohlberg's empirical work, many men reach stage six wherein they could at least engage in rudimentary if not philosophically elegant ways of making universal judgments based on their abstraction from actual moral situations in all of their contextual embeddedness. Women, according to Kohlberg, became stuck at stage three. And what is stage three? It is when a person makes moral and ethical judgments not based on abstract and universal reasoning, but rather by looking only at the concrete and contextual situations under which a given problem arose. This sort of thinking, for Kohlberg, yielded moral judgments that posited, for example, that sometimes it might be right to steal medicine from the pharmacy for your mother, and sometimes it would not be right. This way of thinking, for Kohlberg, correlated with the difference between women and men. To some degree, Gilligan herself also accepted this correlation. And, there has been much ink spilled with respect to the question of to what degree Gilligan actually accepted the correlation. What I want to emphasize is that Gilligan inverted its meaning; she inverted the meaning by asking: What if that way of thinking about ethics was at least equally as good as universal moral codes? And, therefore, *A Different*

Voice claimed that women's moral thinking should be taken seriously as providing humankind with an ethic of care. Gilligan's own claims were rather modest. She at no time argued that an ethic of care should completely displace universal moral thinking, but rather that it should be taken seriously and not degraded simply because it was associated with women. Women's voice of difference, in other words, should finally not only be heard, but more importantly, it should be respected. Many feminists jumped on her argument and proceeded to take it one step further. An ethic of care was indeed better than abstract justice, no matter how conceived, and that women's voice of difference should certainly be respected and heeded, but heeded precisely because it offered a better ethic than the one implied by a misreading of Kant and of one of his respected Anglo-American interpreters, the philosopher John Rawls.[11]

Along with the idea of an ethic of care came a critique of autonomy. Again, not in the Kantian sense but, rather, in the sense of self-determination. Human beings are, so the argument went, relational all the way down. We are fragile creatures born of women and we only have a chance to flourish and survive if we understand ourselves as thoroughly interdependent creatures; not ones who in any other way, but in a fantasy, can be self-determining. This relational view of the self was part and parcel of the ethics of care as many feminists embraced it and elaborated on it. In Seyla Benhabib's groundbreaking book *Situating the Self*,[12] she tried to define the difference by arguing that sometimes we should make judgments as "generalized subjects" and other times as a "situated self." Meanwhile, Marxist feminists continued to cling strongly to the position that the problem was not difference, or even the development of an ethic of care through respect for women's different voices; the problem instead was about the material inequality brought about by capitalism. They further argued that if de Beauvoir's demand that women simply forsake reproduction as utopian, the entire notion of the reproduction of the human species has to be completely reorganized.

In the late 1970s at a conference in the United States, ironically on de Beauvoir's work, an argument broke out between white and African American feminists. The group led by the acclaimed poet and philosopher, Audre Lorde, argued that women of color feminists were simply being ignored, and the questions of anti-Black racism and racism against all people of color had to be confronted if there was to be a meaningful alliance between women of color and white women.[13]

This confrontation led to a major rift within the feminist movement. Moreover, all of the above-mentioned debates became contentious. One of the most profound arguments made by women of color feminists was that even the right to abortion had to be rethought as it existed within the struggle for reproductive freedom that included all the ways in which women of color, against their will, were forced into being the objects of experiments for birth control testing, as well as often persuaded into signing away their right to have children because of forced sterilization. This sterilization often happened to women who depended on welfare.[14] As stated above, de Beauvoir argued that women must forsake motherhood and marriage in the name of their struggle for existential freedom. The argument made by African American women at the conference was that slavery had taken away from women the ability to marry, as well as to claim their own children. Therefore, they were not burdened by motherhood because the option of motherhood itself was something that had been decisively denied to them. In fact, under slavery, if they gave birth at all, they gave birth to "commodities," not to children. And these commodities were simply taken away from them. In the United States, it was not until the mid-twentieth century that interracial marriage was finally allowed and was no longer considered a crime (in South Africa under apartheid it was also a criminal offense). Thus, the argument made by women of color feminists was that there were no race-neutral notions of motherhood, reproductive freedom, or even of marriage. All of these needed to be combated within the greater context of the struggle against anti-Black racism and the struggle for all people of color. I completely accept the criticism of the women of color and agree that the entire program of feminism must be informed by anti-Black racism and the struggle against racism more generally.

How might uBuntu help us think differently about these debates? First, as we have already argued, to advocate for uBuntu as a philosophically important vision of our human being already demands that we fight against anti-Black racism since we are advocating for the philosophical significance of an African ideal or value. Thus, all reform programs of feminism or womanism must incorporate this struggle against anti-Black racism. I call myself an ethical feminist, and at the very core of ethical feminism is the struggle against racism and any other form of degradation that throws some below the bar of the so-called ideals of what it means to be human. Thus, uBuntu thinking can help us think differently about how profound it is that feminism must be raised as anti-racist as part of the definition of ethical feminism. Second, and as this debate is going in reverse order since the context of revolutionary uBuntu has already been described, it implies a different way of thinking about belonging that contests the notion of neoliberal capitalism and the ideology of radical individualism. As previously argued, in the place of radical individualism, we have an understanding of the human being that is always already intertwined in relations that are ethical. The community, however, is not something abstract and outside. It is part of who and how we are with others. It is this intertwinement that makes uBuntu transformative, as there is always more work to do together in shaping our future. The future in a deep sense is always a collective project. But this does not mean that individuation is not valued in uBuntu. As already argued, individuation is indeed valued, but as individuation, not as individuality. Thus the flourishing of one human being is not separate from the flourishing of all others. And, therefore, in this sense, individuation is valued as individuation within the greater context of a collective struggle. The fantasy of a self-contained and self-determining human being is denied. So, in the sense of the European and Anglo-American debates, the self is understood to be relational all the way to the core, and yet each individual will have his or her own unique destiny.

In terms of the debates between the relational self and those who defended the self as a self-determining autonomous self, uBuntu could offer a way out of the paradox by positing that people are only individuated through the support of others, but through this support they do ultimately become unique and singular. Here a different way of thinking about justice and care becomes obvious. As is often underscored in the writings on uBuntu in South Africa, uBuntu can justify the dignity of all others. It does so through our sameness, but in a very different sense. We are all equal before the contingencies, fragility, and finitude of our human being, and therefore we all need care and support if we are to flourish. But we cannot flourish under conditions of inequality that deny that sameness. The focus must be on achieving what we can and should build in common so that all of us can flourish, and not on how we should create a world of self-determining and separated individualities. The radical egalitarianism of revolutionary uBuntu and the different sense of what it means to belong together therefore advocates for a very different way of thinking about justice and care. There can be no justice and, therefore, no respect for the dignity of all others under conditions of inequality. The argument here is that each one of us is different in our very singularity, and I would argue that this demands the opening up of space for new modes of symbolizing the feminine within sexual difference. At the same time, though, it also recognizes the material inequality and oppression of literally millions upon millions of people on this planet, including women and men; this inequality must be overcome as we struggle to build a life in common. Anything less would fly in the face of justice. So there is not a contrast between justice and care. Therefore, they do not need to be pitted against one another but, rather, held as part and parcel of a new way of thinking about our human being that demands there can be no care without justice, and without justice there will be no future wherein all human beings can claim their sameness and a new vision of how human beings can live together on this earth.

Some activists have criticized uBuntu not only for its failure to address economic inequality and the failure of the promised transformation to an egalitarian society rooted in dignity and freedom, but also for uBuntu's failure to address the dreadful attacks on gays, lesbians, and the transgendered. Here I need to stress again that, like all philosophical concepts, the horizon of uBuntu is its future in struggle, because it is a concept that is never settled. Could uBuntu be mobilized against these horrific attacks? Yes, and it must be! But it does not just happen. We need to mobilize and explain why uBuntu is so important for helping take on the project of creating a humanity together that is worthy of its name. It is important to remember that the South African Constitutional Court was one of the first in the world to recognize the full rights of gays and lesbians to marry. The Lesbian and Gay Sangoma Association, an organization of spiritual leaders in South Africa, fought hard to protect the rights of the transgendered because gender binarism is itself challenged by spiritual possession and the role of the ancestors in all our lives.

REVOLUTIONARY BLACK FEMINISM

In chapter 2, I discussed at length how C. L. R. James's understanding of Black liberation is not just the battle against anti-Black racism and white supremacy, as important as that is. Those issues are what Lewis Gordon argues are "liberation from."[15] Gordon rightly makes the distinction between liberation *from* and liberation *to*, as the struggle for Black empowerment is a liberation *to* a transformed world.[16] As early as 1974, the Combahee River Collective, a Black lesbian collective, boldly asserted that the interlocking oppressions of race, class, gender, and heteronormativity demand that capitalism be overthrown. To quote the collective's statement,

> We realize that the liberation of all oppressed peoples necessitates the destruction of the political-economic systems of capitalism and imperialism as well as patriarchy. We are socialists because we believe that work must be organized for the collective benefit of those who do the work and create the products, not for the profit of the bosses. Material resources must be equally distributed among those who create these resources. We are not convinced, however, that a socialist revolution that is not also a feminist and anti-racist revolution will guarantee our liberation. We have arrived at the necessity for developing an understanding of class relationships that take into account the specific class position of Black women who are generally marginal in the labor force, while at this particular time some of us are temporarily viewed as doubly desirable tokens at white-collar and professional levels. We need to articulate the real class situation of persons who are not merely raceless, sexless workers, but for whom racial and sexual oppression are significant determinants in their working/economic lives. Although we are in essential agreement with Marx's theory as it applied to the very specific economic relationships he analyzed, we know that his analysis must be extended further in order for us to understand our specific economic situation as Black women.[17]

In her interview with Barbara Smith (one of the members of the Combahee River Collective), in *How We Get Free*, Keeanga-Yamahtta Taylor emphasizes the importance and centrality of their anti-capitalist and explicitly socialist politics:

> I might not have called what we did "original" Black feminism, but instead wrote that the reason Combahee's Black feminism is so powerful is because it's anticapitalist. One would expect Black feminism to be antiracist and opposed to sexism. Anticapitalism is what gives it the sharpness, the edge, the thoroughness, the revolutionary potential.[18]

If capitalism produces racism—and necessarily so, in the search for ever greater profits through cheap labor and the attacks on all of what so many European countries take for granted as "entitlements": health care as a human right, decent housing, access to good education, free public college, and so on—then the struggle is against racialized capitalism. The Combahee River Collective saw that liberation could only take place through a socialism that ends racialized capitalism. The listed entitlements are not socialism although they would be a big step forward in the United States.

We need to keep in mind the distinction between social democracy and democratic socialism. As we saw in chapter 3 the great experiments in democratic socialism in the Caribbean in the 1970s and 1980s attempted to realize full democratic control over economic institutions by creating a system of interlinked cooperatives rather than nationalization of key resources often associated with socialism. The entire structure of government would change even if some form of parliamentarianism would remain. In Trinidad and Antigua, these were indeed struggles in process. They were daring and, as I wrote in chapter 3, we have so much to learn from these experiments. But what does Black revolutionary feminism add? The insistence that all issues of patriarchy be confronted and that there be a thorough-going challenge to all forms of sexism, including any remnants of homophobia and any oppression against transgender people. This challenge would have to be within revolutionary organizations themselves. Stokely Carmichael, a great revolutionary, once said that the role of women in revolutionary movements was prone. He got that wrong and I write this without debunking his courage and leadership. Much better to have women on their feet and at the heart of the struggle. I write from personal experience as a young woman involved in revolutionary organizations including one that committed itself to armed self-defense of the Black Panther Party. But was there blatant sexism and often contempt for women comrades? Unfortunately, yes. Were there sexist and racist stereotypes often imposed upon our women of color comrades? Again, yes.[19]

bell hooks eloquently elaborates on the complex way sexism and visions of so-called hot women haunt even those who try to provide us with a cultural movement that is anti-racist and anti-sexist. To quote bell hooks:

Throughout the history of white supremacy in the United States, racist white men have regarded the bi-racial white and black female as a sexual ideal. Black men have taken their cues from white men in this regard. Stereotypically portrayed as embodying a passionate sensual eroticism as well as a subordinate feminine nature, the bi-racial–looking black woman as well as the bi-racial woman has been and remains the standard other black females are measured against. Even when darker-skinned black women are given "play" in mass media, television, and movies their characters are usually subordinated to lighter skinned females who are deemed more desirable.[20]

These challenges of how we struggle to make sense of our sexuate being have sometimes been trivialized in revolutionary movements who focus on the struggle for socialism even as these struggles also emphasize Black empowerment. But there should be no hierarchy of importance, which is why throughout this book I have relied on Paget Henry's distinction between the vertical and horizontal aspects of the revolution. Black revolutionary feminists have been exemplary in showing how the two must be brought together if we are to create a world worthy of the humanity we can create together. Again, to quote bell hooks,

There will be no feminist revolution without an end to racism and white supremacy. When all women and men engaged in feminist struggle understand the interlocking nature of systems of domination, of white supremacist capitalist patriarchy, feminist movement will regain its revolutionary progressive momentum.[21]

bell hooks also exemplifies the insistence on the return of spirituality to revolutionary struggle. In all her work, including her memoirs through her three books on love, she was fearless in insisting on the centrality of spirituality to individual and collective transformation. Of course, as important as her work is, bell hooks is not alone in her emphasis on spirituality and what we have been referring to as the vertical revolution, following Paget Henry. Audre Lorde famously connects her queer sexuality to a spirituality rooted in the body but irreducible to it. Spirituality as embodied is a crucial aspect of love with its transformative power. She writes,

It has become fashionable to separate the spiritual (psychic and emotional) from the political, to see them as contradictory or antithetical.

"What do you mean, a poetic revolutionary, a meditating gunrunner?" In the same way, we have attempted to separate the spiritual and the erotic, thereby reducing the spiritual to a world of flattened affect, a world of the ascetic who aspires to feel nothing. . . . The dichotomy between the spiritual and the political is also false, resulting from an incomplete attention to our erotic knowledge. For the bridge which connects them is formed by the erotic—the sensual—those physical, emotional, and psychic expressions of what is deepest and strongest and richest within each of us, being shared: the passions of love, in its deepest meanings.[22]

bell hooks, in her trilogy on love, returns again and again to love as a joyous sharing of our world together.[23] This vision of love and spirituality challenges the divide between the material and the spiritual that has haunted the history of hard-core Marxists that insisted that dialectical materialism is truth in science and therefore cannot be challenged.

In *When They Call Us Terrorists*, Patrice Khan-Cullors celebrates the stardust people in her family who survived the most horrific and cruel forms of racism. She knew that her family had the magic of stardust from her own experience with them. As she writes,

And I knew it because I am the thirteenth-generation progeny of a people who survived the hulls of slave ships, survived the chains, the whips, the months laying in their own shit and piss. The human beings legislated as not human beings who watched their names, their languages, their Goddesses and Gods, the arc of their dances and beats of their songs, the majesty of their dreams, their very families snatched up and stolen, disassembled and discarded, and despite this built language and honored God and created movement and upheld love. What could they be but stardust, these people who refused to die, who refused to accept the idea that their lives did not matter, that their children's lives did not matter?

Our foreparents imagined our families out of whole cloth. They imagined each individual one of us. They imagined me. They had to. It was the only way I am here, today, a mother and a wife, a community organizer and Queer, an artist and a dreamer learning to find hope while navigating the shadows of hell even as I know it might have been otherwise.[24]

She knows that her brother Paul is regularly harassed and beaten on the street, and so is her brother Monte. They never spoke about it, "They will not discuss it with me, who was a witness, or my mother, who was not. They will not be outraged. They will not say they do not deserve such treatment. Because by the time they hit puberty, neither will my brothers have expected that things could be another way."[25] That was their crime, that they were Black and on the street. This is what the philosopher Lewis Gordon calls hypervisibility. To quote Gordon,

> The presumption is that even if many blacks didn't commit the crime of which they are accused, they must be guilty of something. Choose any crime except for individually enacted mass homicide, on which white men have a near monopoly, and there are too many black people involved—because there are too many black people around in the first place.[26]

Both Khan-Cullors's father Gabriel and her brother Monte were imprisoned. Monte was diagnosed with schizophrenia. He received no mental care when he was first in prison. Out of prison, his was a heartbreaking struggle with his illness of course he did not understand. It took him and his world over. The sorrow over Monte's fate left his mother, Cherice, in tears, which was the only times Khan-Cullors saw her mother cry. Bernard, a family friend and ultimately Cherice's husband, gets Monte into a hospital where he is stabilized. But the family's tragedy is far from over. Later on, Monte is arrested again as a terrorist, denied treatment, and put in solitary confinement in a high-security prison. The public defender does not do his job. The family hires a lawyer who cuts a deal, but Monte must serve out the rest of his six-year sentence, of course completely traumatized by the treatment of his jailers. Gabriel, Khan-Cullors's beloved father, does not return to prison but tragically dies. He struggled with cocaine addiction but no reason is given for his death, just that it was not foul play. Khan-Cullors writes of her father,

> We sit before his casket as "Taps" begins to play and a soldier presents me with the folded American flag that had covered his coffin. I take it and I hold it, this flag for a nation in which my father, my Black father, my good and imperfect and loving Black father, could not be possible.
>
> My father who got cages instead of compassion.
>
> My father whose whole story no one of us will ever know.
>
> What did it do to him, all those years locked away, all that time in chains, all those days upon days without human touch expect touch meant to harm—*hands behind your back, N*****. Get on the fucking wall,*

> N*****! Lift your sac, N*****. Don't look at me like that or I will fucking kill your Black ass.

> It would be easy to speculate about the impact of years of cocaine use on my father's heart, but I suspect that it will tell us less than if we could measure the cumulative effects of hatred, racism and indignity. What is the impact of years of strip searches, of being bent over, the years before that when you were a child and knew that no dream you had for yourself was taken seriously by anyone, that you were not someone who would be fully invested in by a nation that treated you as expendable?[27]

Khan-Cullors became an activist at the age of 16 and was in the trenches for years before becoming one of the three women to adopt the hashtag "BlackLivesMatter" for a movement that has shaken countries throughout the world. What she developed out of her own experience is called Black consciousness. As Gordon tells us, no one is born with Black consciousness. Black consciousness grows out of racism and the experience of dehumanization it imposes. What Khan-Cullors powerfully describes is linked to what Gordon calls her Black consciousness. Again, to quote Gordon as I did in the introduction,

> Whereas black consciousness may be linked to the role consigned to the black person in an antiblack society, Black consciousness is organically linked to what black and all people ultimately need: the transformation of the society that produces antiblack racism and other kinds of dehumanization into something better. Black consciousness is linked to building a better world to come. This is the quest for liberation. As liberation would require a radical change of society, we could also call it a revolution.[28]

Her continuous activism leads her to Black consciousness, which underwrites her life as a freedom fighter. Black Lives Matter exemplifies Black empowerment. To quote Gordon,

> Racism is the channeling of institutional mechanisms of power toward the disempowerment of targeted groups of people; its effectiveness depends on the meeting of state and cultural resources. People bring legitimacy to their society's formal aspirations. When a sufficient number of people oppose problematic formal social mechanisms and create alternative ones, others with stubborn individual attachments to the past become irrelevant. That is the ultimate fear of racists—their own irrelevance. As their relevance depends on a society wedded to racism, the empowerment of those

they would exclude sounds the death knell of the racist system. And since systems can be built and sustained only by people, Black empowerment should be the goal of anyone committed to eradicating antiblack racism and other kinds of degradation of what it means to be human.[29]

CREOLE METAPHYSICS AND CREOLIZATION

There is another aspect of the writings of the revolutionary Black feminists I have cited, which at least implicitly engages with what Paget Henry defines as the creole tradition. For Henry, the creole tradition grows out of the experience of forced mixing that was imposed by European colonizers. From within this tradition, a specific metaphysics grows that Henry names creative realism. To quote Henry,

> Yet another distinguishing feature of the Caribbean creole tradition is the distinct underlying metaphysics upon which it rests. I have called this metaphysics *creative realism*. At the heart of creative realism are four foundational claims. First, that the violence of European colonization shattered the integrated nature of all four cultural traditions it forced to mix with each other within the Caribbean context. Second, that with this splintering or fragmenting of these traditions, the members of these dominated and imploded cultures no longer inherited culturally established definitions of themselves such as Akan, Yoruba, Hindu, or Islamic. Along with the fragments of these earlier identities, they now experienced more directly the inherent creativity of the human self by which those more holistic identities where produced. Third, that the implosions produced by this forced mixing released seismic shock waves that severely rocked the founding centers of these cultural systems. These founding centers rested on varying notions of spirit, which were seen as the ultimate creative sources, and thus the highest of realities. This central position of spirit became much more open to contestation in the course of these forced mixings. Fourth and finally, the inherent creativity exposed by these mixings, although very energetic, was capable only of provisional solutions to crucial existential problems, or what Wilson Harris called "rehearsals" (1993). In short, creative realism rested and continues to rest on a de-centered metaphysics that permits competing perspectives to provisionally occupy the center, but never in a genuinely final sense. It is a metaphysics that described and continues to describe the new existential address of the Caribbean subject, somewhere between pr-colonial classical traditions

and the imperatives of European modernity brought on by the experience of colonization.[30]

None of the writers I have quoted explicitly write from out of the metaphysics of the Caribbean. So why am I saying that their work expresses some of the key aspects of creative realism? Creative realism may have originated in the experience of hybridization in the Caribbean but its reach is not reduced to its locale of origin. Indeed, the whole practice of what has now become known as creolizing rejects localism in the name of a universal reach of revolutionary theory and practice. Key concepts in philosophy such as the subject have been creolized, as have been the work of key thinkers in Euro-United States philosophy including a book I coedited titled *Creolizing Rosa Luxemburg*.[31]

How does a Caribbean tradition travel? In a profound sense, the same question has been asked of African philosophy. If Afro-Caribbean philosophy and African philosophy have a justification in the universal that no longer assumes Euro-American concepts are the universal, then we can see the importance of shifting the geographies of reason in uBuntu feminism, revolutionary black feminism, and, yes, creative realism. Of course, anything like a full elaboration of the connection between African philosophy and revolutionary Black feminism is way beyond the scope of this book, but over many years now we have seen the power of connecting and recognizing differences as part of a rethinking the universal outside Eurocentrism. But let's for a moment return to a possible way of thinking the connection between revolutionary Black feminism and creative realism and the return of spirituality to revolutionary philosophy.

What we have seen in black revolutionary feminism is precisely the working through of complex identity. In both Lorde and Khan-Cullors's works, what it means to be a Black queer woman committed to activism is seen as explicit in the project of becoming a revolutionary. As we have also seen, returning to Henry's idea of creole metaphysics, the attention to the spiritual, including love, as what Wilson Harris[32] calls a rehearsal of a new way of being human together, is also crucial to Black revolutionary feminism. Stephen Seeley and I justified political spirituality as itself a creolization of Michel Foucault who first used the expression in reference to Iran.[33] Political spirituality explicitly recognizes how "spirit" infuses new visions and practices of the human. These rehearsals, to use Wilson Harris's phrase, and experiments can always be transformed as the demands of justices and dignity change in the course of revolutionary struggles.

Political spirituality is not as personal as love and spirituality in, for example, Audre Lorde, bell hooks, and Khan-Cullors. It goes more to what Lewis Gordon calls political responsibility.[34] Part of our responsibility, even in revolutionary struggles, is to recognize the importance of rehearsals but not freeze them into moral certitude, let alone scientific truths that were often acclaimed as the work of dialectical materialism. Creative realism and African philosophy open up new vistas of revolutionary thought. As we have seen with the work of creolization, the journey is to liberate thought and practice and not simply to engage in an endless critique of the limits of Eurocentrism. Feminism and gay and lesbian and transgendered experiences have shown how crucial it is to challenge how we live together in our so-called personal lives. There is no means to an end but constant transformation as we try to live out the ideals which inspire us to activism.

Conclusion

Tomorrow's Revolution: A Call to Action in Salvador Allende's Last Words

When Salvador Allende was elected president of Chile, young socialists around the world cheered. Yes, Allende was a socialist, but he was committed to democracy. The dream of democratic socialism was no longer just a utopian longing but coming to be in an actual country. In his brief reign as president, some of the most difficult problems of the horizontal revolution were being addressed. What it means to successfully transform the economy so that people had democratic control of all economic institutions was being implemented. As we saw in chapter 3, some of the most daring attempts to create democratic cooperatives, run collectively by the workers, were developed in the Caribbean. In Antigua and Trinidad, C. L. R. James's notion of a radical participatory economic organization was taken seriously, and cooperatives run by the workers were created. Of course, there were problems as there will always be if we truly attempt to radically transform economic relations and end the exploitation that inheres in capitalist modes of production. These problems and the failure of many cooperatives to survive do not mean that we do not have a lot to learn from both them and the visionary leadership of someone like Tim Hector. We need to think seriously about those efforts, which is why I turned to them in chapter 3. But in Antigua and Trinidad, the visionary democratic socialist organizations did not take state power. In Chile, Allende took power through an election. His election changed the face of what a socialist revolution could look like. It was no longer taking the state through armed struggle, as happened in Cuba. We all remember that historic moment when Fidel

Castro and Che Guevara marched into Havana. The history of Cuba, including its current acceptance of certain market reforms, is extremely complicated and clearly beyond the scope of this book.

It was a different world. The Soviet Union still existed and was a world power. Many revolutionary movements turned to the Soviet Union for support, including arms and training, as did the African National Congress of South Africa. Cuba was itself dependent on that support. What was clear was that the United States set out to overthrow the new Cuban government as soon as it was established. Under President John F. Kennedy, there was an armed invasion, which was called the Bay of Pigs, that was a complete failure. Then there was the Cuban missile crisis, because the Soviet Union had placed nuclear warheads in Cuba. This crisis brought us very close to a third world war. That crisis was part of the Cold War more generally. I was raised in an anti-Communist frenzy because of that Cold War. We were threatened by "them" and Cuba was right at the heart of that threat. After the Bay of Pigs failed, Fidel miraculously survived innumerable assassination attempts, dying at a ripe old age. I do not want to deny any of Cuba's important achievements. The country has one of the highest literacy rates in the world. It has an outstanding health system both in terms of delivery and research. Most recently, their research scientists have created their own vaccine for COVID-19 which proceeds differently from those of the likes of Moderna and Pfizer, and Cuba is now distributing that vaccine for free to many African countries. In Cuba you do not have to worry about being bankrupted if you get sick or need, God forbid, dental work. Bernie Sanders's big dream of old people being able to see and hear their grandchildren and have teeth to eat with them—a dream he has fought to realize in his constant call for Medicare for all—has long since been realized in Cuba.

But for all of Cuba's continuing accomplishments, the revolution was from a different era. Fidel instituted what he thought was the dictatorship of the proletariat. For all of Che Guevara's heroism, he took a small group of armed men into the rural areas of South America, thinking they could create a revolution. Tragically, he died for his heroism and his idealism. The dictatorship of the proletariat in Cuba led to many oppressions that many of us socialists rejected while fighting militantly against the embargo and the refusal to see what Cuba accomplished. But then there was Allende, who refused to think that armed struggle was the only way to seize state power. He was elected as a democratic socialist. Those of us who rejected the dictatorship of the proletariat saw a new means of revolution. Democracy and grassroots organizing could bring democratic socialism to the government. Indeed, this government could implement that complicated work of the horizontal revolution. We were elated. Here revolution had a different face from the dominance of the model of the Soviet Union, and it was really happening. Now democratic socialism was both a means and an end!

Tragically, the United States made it clear that they were not only opposed to Allende but determined to bring him down. In his beautifully written and deeply moving book, *Story of Death Foretold*, Oscar Guardiola-Rivera takes us painfully through how the United States played a central role in the coup against the Allende government. Of course, Guardiola-Rivera also reviews for us that the United States has had a bloody history in South America, overturning by violence one revolutionary movement after another. Leaders were assassinated or forced to step down. It is a shameful imperialist history. As we discussed in chapter 2, Rosa Luxemburg writes that at the end of the day we will have to choose between socialism or barbarism, and this was barbaric indeed. The coup that fell Allende led to Augusto Pinochet's seizure of the reins of power through terror, killing or disappearing of thousands of people. Economists from the reactionary school of the University of Chicago jumped in to support Pinochet, to help restore capitalism and became advisors to his regime. What this shows is that there is a fragile relationship between capitalism and basic democratic freedoms, and this was exposed for all to see given the support of US economists for the Pinochet regime. But Allende did not go quietly. He refused to surrender. To quote his last words,

> I shall not surrender! Placed at a historical crossroads, I shall pay with my life for your loyalty, the loyalty of the people. And I tell you with complete certainty, that the seed I put today in your hands and plant in the untainted soul and the worthy memory of thousands upon thousands of Chileans will not be uprooted ever. They are strong, they can defeat us, but the movement of society cannot be stopped by either crime or force. History is ours, and the people make it. Workers of Chile: I thank you for your fidelity, the trust you have placed in a man who was merely an interpreter of your deep yearnings for justice, who pledged his words to defend the law and the constitution, and who has kept it.[1]

He saw what was coming: the horrifying violence of Pinochet's outright fascism. Again, to quote Allende,

> Workers of my land, the land of our fathers, I believe in Chile and its destiny. Other men shall overcome this grey and bitter moment in which treachery claims the upper hand. You will keep going, knowing that sooner rather than later the great avenues will open up once more, through which free men will walk on, to build a better society.
>
> Long live Chile! Long live the people! Long live the workers! These are my final words. I am certain that my sacrifice will not be in vain. I am certain that, at the very least, it shall serve as a moral judgment on the felony, cowardice and treason that lay waste to our land.[2]

It was September 11, 1973. A man committed to constitutionalism and a peaceful transition to democratic socialism took on an army in the name of the ideals to which he had committed his life. Thousands of young activists poured into the Sheep Meadow in Central Park. To grieve? Yes! But to recommit to the seeds that had been planted and would not be uprooted. It would be up to us. As Guardiola-Rivera tells us, "Allende spoke with his sights fixed on the future. His words were left to those who would hear them forty years later."[3] I heard Allende's words then and they echo with me now, whenever I am tempted by despair. The Caribbean thinkers as well as other revolutionary thinkers who are at the heart of this book tell us that there is only one real choice, and that is to fight on for a just world worthy of our humanity. For me, the power of Allende's call has stayed with me all these years later and in a deep sense inspired me to write this book.

Notes

INTRODUCTION

1. Solomon J. Terreblanche, *Inequality in South Africa, 1652–2002* (Pietermaritzburg: University of Natal Press, 2002).
2. Solomon J. Terreblanche, *Lost in Transformation: South Africa's Search for a New Future Since 1986* (Johannesburg: KMM Review Publishing Company, 2012).
3. See Paget Henry, *Caliban's Reason: Introducing Afro-Caribbean Philosophy* (New York: Routledge, 2000).
4. See generally Frantz Fanon, *The Wretched of the Earth*, trans. Richard Philcox (New York: Grove Press, 2004).
5. See generally Drucilla Cornell, *The Philosophy of the Limit* (New York: Routledge, 1992).
6. Lewis Gordon, *Fear of Black Consciousness* (New York: Farrar, Straus and Giroux, 2022).
7. Toni Morrison, *The Source of Self-Regard: Selected Essays, Speeches, and Meditations* (New York: Alfred A. Knopf, 2019), 18.

8. (1) Construct an internal enemy, as both focus and diversion. (2) Isolate and demonize that enemy by unleashing and protecting the utterance of overt and coded name-calling and verbal abuse. Employ ad hominem attacks as legitimate charges against that enemy. (3) Enlist and create sources and distributors of information who are willing to reinforce the demonizing process because it is profitable, because it grants power, and because it works. (4) Palisade all art forms; monitor, discredit, or expel those that challenge or destabilize processes of demonization and deification. (5) Subvert and malign all representatives of and sympathizers with this constructed enemy. (6) Solicit, from among the enemy, collaborators who

agree with and can sanitize the dispossession process. (7) Pathologize the enemy in scholarly and popular mediums; recycle, for example, scientific racism and the myths of racial superiority in order to naturalize the pathology. (8) Criminalize the enemy. Then prepare, budget for, and rationalize the building of holding arenas for the enemy—especially in males and absolutely its children. (9) Reward mindlessness and apathy with monumentalized entertainments and with little pleasures, tiny seductions: a few minutes on television, a few lines in the press; a little pseudo-success; the illusion of power and influence; a little fun, a little style a little consequence. (10) Maintain, at all costs, silence. (Ibid., 18–19).

9. Ibid., 20–21.
10. Ibram X. Kendi, *How to Be an Antiracist* (New York: Random House, 2019).
11. See Drucilla Cornell, *Between Women and Generations: Legacies of Dignity* (Lanham, MD: Rowman & Littlefield, 2005).
12. *Brown v. Board of Education*, 347 U.S. 483. (1953).
13. Michael P. MacDonald, *All Souls: A Family Story from Southie* (Boston: Beacon Press, 1999).
14. See Noel Ignatiev, *How the Irish Became White* (New York: Routledge, 1995).
15. See the Massachusetts Racial Imbalance Act. *Barksdale v. Springfield School Committee*, 237 F. Supp. 543 (D. Mass. 1965).

CHAPTER 1

1. "Fatal Force: Police Shootings Database," *The Washington Post*, January 22, 2020, https://www.washingtonpost.com/graphics/investigations/police-shootings-database/.
2. Larry Buchanan, Quoctrung Bui, and Jugai K. Patel, "Black Lives Matter May Be the Largest Movement in US History," *New York Times*, July 3, 2020, https://www.nytimes.com/interactive/2020/07/03/us/george-floyd-protests-crowd-size.html.
3. "Black Lives Matter Protests 2020 (Interactive Map)," accessed July 5, 2020, https://www.creosotemaps.com/blm2020/index.html.
4. See Part II of Thomas Hobbes, *Leviathan* (New York: Penguin, 1985) and Max Weber, "The Profession and Vocation of Politics," in *Political Writings*, eds. Peter Lassman and Ronald Speirs (Cambridge: Cambridge University Press, 1994), 310–11. As Étienne Balibar details, European political philosophy begins from an understanding of social relations as "naturally" antagonistic and violent, from which the state emerges as a form of "preventive *counter-violence*"—or, following Hegel, a "conversion" of violence—that

maintains social order and security only by using the threat of violence to keep the originary violence of the "state of nature" in check (see Étienne Balibar, *Violence and Civility: On the Limits of Political Philosophy*, trans. G. M. Goshgarian [New York: Columbia University Press, 2016]). I agree with Balibar's conclusion that within such a context "non-violence" is simply a theoretical abstraction, and I will return to his notion of "anti-violence" shortly, but I also want to point out that if one looks beyond Europe there are many other social ontologies, such as *uBuntu*, which do not begin from the understanding of relations as intrinsically antagonistic or violent.

5. See John Locke, *Two Treatises of Government*, ed. Peter Laslett (Cambridge: Cambridge University Press, 1988).

6. Brenna Bhandar, *Colonial Lives of Property: Law, Land, and Racial Regimes of Ownership* (Durham NC: Duke University Press, 2018).

7. In her genealogy of self-defense, French philosopher Elsa Dorlin argues that the fundamental political division is those who have lives and bodies worth defending and those who do not, and that the "organization of disarmament" is precisely the way in which racial-colonial hegemony is maintained. See Elsa Dorlin, *Se Défendre: Une Philosophie de la Violence* (Paris: La Découverte Poche, 2019).

8. See Mahmood Mamdani, *Good Muslim, Bad Muslim: America, the Cold War, and the Roots of Terror* (New York: Pantheon, 2004).

9. Balibar, *Violence and Civility*.

10. See Michel Foucault, "Useless to Revolt?" in *Power (The Essential Works of Foucault, 1954–1984, Vol. 3)*, ed. James B. Faubion (New York: The New Press, 2001), 449–53.

11. Hannah Arendt, "On Violence," in *Crises of the Republic* (New York: Harcourt Brace & Co., 1972), 143, 145.

12. See Hannah Arendt, *The Human Condition* (Chicago: University of Chicago Press, 1958).

13. Arendt, "On Violence," 155.

14. Ibid., 132.

15. For more on this, see Hannah Arendt, *On Revolution* (New York: Penguin, 1963).

16. Arendt, "On Violence," 152.

17. Balibar, *Violence and Civility*. Balibar takes the phrase "disposable human beings" from Bertrand Ogilvie's *L'Homme jetable: Essai sur l'exterminisme et la violence extrême* (Paris: Éditions Amsterdam, 2012), but see also Kevin Bales, *Disposable People: New Slavery in the Global Economy* (Berkeley: University of California Press, 2012).

18. See Joao Biehl, *Vita: Life in a Zone of Social Abandonment* (Berkeley: University of California Press, 2005); Rob Nixon, *Slow Violence and the Environmentalism of the Poor* (Cambridge: Harvard University Press, 2013); Jasbir

Puar, *The Right to Maim: Debility, Capacity, Disability* (Durham, NC: Duke University Press, 2017); Achille Mbembe, *Necropolitics* (Durham, NC: Duke University Press, 2019); Peter Hudis, *Frantz Fanon: Philosopher of the Barricades* (London: Pluto Press, 2015).

19. Balibar, *Violence and Civility*, 69.
20. See Lewis Gordon, *What Fanon Said: A Philosophical Introduction to His Thought and Life* (New York: Fordham University Press, 2015), 121–22.
21. Arendt, "On Violence," 123.
22. Gordon, *What Fanon Said*, 124.
23. Arendt, "On Violence," 184.
24. See Gordon, *What Fanon Said*, 75–105.
25. See Arendt, "On Violence," 155.
26. Ibid., 148. She associates, for instance, the "Black violence" of the 1960s with the "violence" of earlier generations of the labor movement (ibid., 121).
27. Ibid., 161.
28. Ibid., 155.
29. Frantz Fanon, *The Wretched of the Earth*, trans. Richard Philcox (New York: Grove Press, 2004), 2.
30. Aimé Césaire, *Discourse on Colonialism*, trans. Joan Pinkham (New York: Monthly Review Press, 2000), 42.
31. Fanon, *Wretched of the Earth*, 2.
32. Arendt, "On Violence," 179. Emphasis modified.
33. Angela Y. Davis, *Freedom Is a Constant Struggle: Ferguson, Palestine, and the Foundations of a Movement* (Chicago: Haymarket Books, 2016), 89.
34. Arendt, "On Violence," 169.
35. Ibid., 121.
36. Angela Davis, interview by Göran Olsson, *The Black Power Mixtape 1967–1975*.
37. Fanon, *Wretched of the Earth*, 42, 47.
38. Balibar, *Violence and Civility*, 23–24.
39. Ibid., 24.
40. "Insurrection," for Balibar, is the "active modality" of politics—the interruptive demand for equality and liberty (or "equaliberty") by those who have no share in a given order—which must be balanced with "constitution," as the *institutionalization* of the insurrectional demands. See Étienne Balibar, *Citizenship*, trans. Thomas Schott-Railton (Cambridge: Polity, 2015).
41. Civility, for Balibar, is the opposite of cruelty. Balibar is careful to distinguish civility (*civilité*) from notions of *civilization* and *politeness* by emphasizing its etymological roots in the Latin *civilitas*, itself from the Greek *politeia*: civility is thus synonymous with *politics*, *citizenship*, and *political community* (*Violence and Civility*, 23).
42. Fanon, *Wretched of the Earth*, 31.

43. See Martin Luther King Jr. "Showdown for Nonviolence," in *A Testament of Hope: The Essential Writings and Speeches of Martin Luther King Jr.*, ed. James Melvin Washington (San Francisco: HarperCollins, 1986), 64–72.

44. Malcolm X, *The Autobiography of Malcolm X as Told to Alex Haley* (New York: Ballantine Books, 1973), 385.

45. Huey P. Newton, "The Ten-Point Program," in *To Die for the People*, ed. Toni Morrison (San Francisco: City Lights, 2009), 5.

46. Huey P. Newton, "Reply to William Patterson: September 19, 1970," in *To Die for the People*, ed. Toni Morrison (San Francisco: City Lights, 2009), 177–78. Emphasis added.

47. See "About RAWA . . . ," *Revolutionary Afghan Women's Association*. Accessed July 5, 2020. http://www.rawa.org/rawa.html.

48. Fanon, *Wretched of the Earth*, 42.

49. See Drucilla Cornell and Karin van Marle, *Albie Sachs and Transformation in South Africa: From Revolutionary Activist to Constitutional Court Judge* (Oxford: Birkbeck Law Press, 2014).

50. See Drucilla Cornell, *Law and Revolution in South Africa: uBuntu, Dignity, and the Struggle for Constitutional Transformation* (New York: Fordham University Press, 2014).

51. Cornell and van Marle, *Albie Sachs*, 80.

52. Balibar, *Citizenship*, 131.

53. Fanon, *Wretched of the Earth*, 239.

CHAPTER 2

1. Wendy Brown, "Women's Studies Unbound: Revolution, Mourning, Politics," *Parallax* 9, no. 2 (2003): 13.

2. Alain Badiou, *The Communist Hypothesis*, trans. David Macey and Steve Corcoran (London: Verso, 2010).

3. Lewis Gordon, *Freedom, Justice, and Decolonization* (New York: Routledge, 2021), 23.

4. Ibid.

5. Frantz Fanon, *The Wretched of the Earth*, trans. Richard Philcox (New York: Grove Press, 2004).

6. See chapter 3 of Gordon's *Freedom, Justice, and Decolonization* and Frantz Fanon, *A Dying Colonialism* (New York: Grove Press, 1967).

7. Gordon, *Freedom, Justice, and Decolonization*, 69.

8. Rosa Luxemburg, *The Russian Revolution*, trans. Bertram D. Wolfe, in *The Rosa Luxemburg Reader*, eds. Peter Hudis and Kevin B. Anderson (New York: Monthly Review Press, 2004), 305–6.

9. See Henri Bergson, *Creative Evolution*, trans. Arthur Mitchell (Mineola: Dover, 1998).

10. Luxemburg, *The Russian Revolution*, 307.

11. Of course, given her stress on creativity, I can argue that a notion of imagination is central to her understanding of revolution, yet she never focused explicitly on the imagination.

12. This is reading between the *Critique of Pure Reason* and the *Critique of Judgement*. For a more detailed version, see the first chapter of Drucilla Cornell, *Moral Images of Freedom: A Future for Critical Theory* (Lanham, MD: Rowman & Littlefield, 2008), 11–38.

13. Herbert Marcuse, *Reason and Revolution: Hegel and the Rise of Social Theory* (Amherst, MA: Humanity Books, 1999).

14. See Orlando Patterson, *Freedom: Freedom in the Making of Western Culture* (New York: Basic Books, 1991).

15. I have written about this interplay elsewhere, drawing on Spinoza, in Drucilla Cornell and Stephen D. Seely, "What Has Happened to the Public Imagination, and Why?" *global-e*, March 21, 2017. https://www.21global.ucsb.edu/global-e/march-2017/what-has-happened-public-imagination-and-why, accessed July 14, 2020.

16. Étienne Balibar, "The Idea of Revolution: Yesterday, Today, and Tomorrow," *Modalities of Revolt* Seminar Series, Columbia Center for Contemporary Critical Thought, August 27, 2017, http://blogs.law.columbia.edu/uprising1313/etienne-balibar-the-idea-of-revolution-yesterday-today-and-tomorrow/, accessed July 14, 2020.

17. Drucilla Cornell and Stephen D. Seely, *The Spirit of Revolution: Beyond the Dead Ends of Man* (Cambridge: Polity, 2016).

18. Ibid.

19. Rosa Luxemburg, *The Mass Strike, the Political Party, and the Trade Unions*, trans. Patrick Lavan, in *The Rosa Luxemburg Reader*, 173.

20. See Abraham Asher, *The Revolution of 1905: A Short History* (Stanford: Stanford University Press, 2004).

21. Luxemburg, *The Mass Strike*, 174–75.

22. Ibid., 180.

23. Ibid., 182.

24. Ibid., 186.

25. Ibid., 192.

26. Ibid., 195.

27. Rosa Luxemburg, *Organizational Questions of Russian Social Democracy*, trans. Richard Taylor, in *The Rosa Luxemburg Reader*, 265.

28. C. L. R. James, "Letters on Politics," in *The C. L. R. James Reader*, ed. Anna Grimshaw (London: Wiley Blackwell, 1992), 272.

29. Ibid., 272–3.

30. Ibid., 272.
31. Ibid., 275.
32. C. L. R. James, "The Revolutionary Answer to the Negro Problem in the US," in *The C. L. R. James Reader*.
33. C. L. R. James, "Black Power," in *The C. L. R. James Reader*, 368.
34. Ibid., 369.
35. C. L. R. James, "Black People in Urban Areas in the United States," in *The C. L. R. James Reader*, 377.
36. C. L. R. James, *Nkrumah and the Ghana Revolution* (Westport, CT: Lawrence Hill & Co., 1977), 57.
37. James, "Black Power," 367.
38. Ibid., 374.
39. C. L. R. James, "Dialectical Materialism and the Fate of Humanity," in *The C. L. R James Reader*.
40. Jean-Paul Sartre, "Black Orpheus," trans. John MacCombie, *The Massachusetts Review* 6, no. 1 (Autumn 1964–Winter 1965), 52.
41. See Drucilla Cornell and Jane Anna Gordon, eds., *Creolizing Rosa Luxemburg* (Lanham, MD: Rowan & Littlefield, 2021).
42. See Paget Henry, "Africana Philosophy and the Possibility of a Third Reconstruction." Pioneers of Africana Philosophy, CUNY Graduate Center for the Humanities (Zoom lecture, March 20, 2021).
43. See W. E. B. Du Bois, *Black Reconstruction in America, 1860–1880* (New York: Harcourt, Brace, 1938).
44. James, "Revolutionary Answer to Negro Problem," 184.

CHAPTER 3

1. See Jean Comaroff and John Comaroff, *Theory from the South; Or, How Euro-America Is Evolving toward Africa* (Boulder: Paradigm, 2012).
2. Jodi Dean, *Crowds and Party* (London: Verso, 2016).
3. Lenin, "R. A Few Words on Dialectics. Two Revolutions." *One Step Forward, Two Steps Back*, Marxists Internet Archive, 277, https://www.marxists.org/archive/lenin/works/1904/onestep/r.htm, accessed May 2, 2022.
4. Ibid., 276.
5. Vladimir Lenin, "The Economic Basis of the Withering Away of the State," *The State and Revolution*, 75,https://www.marxists.org/archive/lenin/works/1917/staterev/ch05.htm, accessed May 2, 2022.
6. Ibid., 80.
7. Ibid., 91.

8. C. L. R. James, *Notes on Dialectics* (Westport, CT: Lawrence Hill & Co., 1981), 173.

9. C. L. R. James, "Dialectical Materialism and the Fate of Humanity," in *The C. L. R. James Reader.*

10. James, *Notes on Dialectics*, 176.

11. But for Sylvia Wynter all humans do this, they just attribute it to supernatural/extrahuman ("natural") agencies. So, communism in this sense is a new praxis of being human that secures what she calls the non-opacity of being, where we create what it means to be human *and are aware that we are doing so* (sociogenic turn).

12. James, *Notes on Dialectics*, 28.

13. Ibid., 142.

14. Ibid., 180. To reinforce James's understanding that *State and Revolution* is no longer the ideal of socialism, I return to James's own words:

> You have a notion. That notion is *State and Revolution*. That governs *everything*. There is no solution to the problems of society except every cook and every worker to a man administers the state and the economy. That is what Lenin means by the proletarian revolution. Perhaps you have it, perhaps not. (I don't want to insult anybody but I mean what I say.) Without *that* you get fascism, imperialist war, barbarism of all kinds. Precisely because *that* is inherent in society, all the barbarism and the evil inherent in human society will emerge also. That is the greatest truth of our time, but we have dealt with that in *Dialectical Materialism and the Fate of Humanity*. (Ibid.)

15. Ibid., 175–76.
16. Ibid., 233–34.
17. Ibid., 76.
18. Ibid., 145.
19. Ibid., 225.
20. Paget Henry, "C. L. R. James, Africana Transcendental Philosophy, and the Creolizing of Hegel," in *Creolizing Hegel*, ed. Michael Monahan (Lanham, MD: Rowman & Littlefield, 2017), 43.
21. Ibid., 48.
22. James, *Notes on Dialectics*, 128.
23. Paget Henry, *Caliban's Reason: Introducing Afro-Caribbean Philosophy* (New York: Routledge, 2000), 121, and Cornell and Seely, *The Spirit of Revolution: Beyond the Dead Ends of Man* (Cambridge: Polity, 2016).
24. C. L. R. James, *You Don't Play with Revolution: The Montreal Lectures of C. L. R. James*, ed. David Austin (Edinburgh: AK Press, 2009), 181.
25. Ibid., 184.

26. Franklyn V. P. Harvey, *Rise and Fall of Party Politics in Trinidad and Tobago* (New Beginnings Movement, 1974).

27. Mathew Quest, "New Beginning Movement," in *The C. L. R. James Journal* 23, no. 1 (2017): 267–305, https://doi.org/10.5840/clrjames2017111642.

28. Ibid.

29. See Souleymane Bachir Diagne, "A Humanism and a Politics of *UBuntu* and *Nite*," Pioneers of Africana Philosophy, CUNY Graduate Center for the Humanities (Zoom lecture, March 20, 2021).

30. See Drucilla Cornell, *Law and Revolution in South Africa: uBuntu, Dignity, and the Struggle for Constitutional Transformation* (New York: Fordham University Press, 2014).

31. Souleymane Bachir Diagne, "A Humanism and a Politics of *UBuntu* and *Nite*."

32. For a full discussion of VC Bird's attempt at Black democratic socialism and why it failed, see Paget Henry, *VC Bird* (London: Hansib, 2010).

33. Tim Hector, *Antigua and Barbuda Review of Books*, vol. 8, no. 1, ed. Paget Henry (Antigua and Babuda Studies Association, 2015), 15.

34. See Paget Henry, *Peripheral Capitalism and Underdevelopment in Antigua* (New Brunswick, NJ: Transaction Books, 1985).

35. Paget Henry, "The Socialist Legacy of Tim Hector," in *Antigua and Barbuda Review of Books*, 112–13.

36. Ibid., 113.

37. Henry offers us a careful analysis of how Hector, who left us in 2002, saw how the globalization of finance capital in the specific form of the twenty-first century intensified the exploitation and disempowerment of the vast majority of people, creating ever new and increasingly frightening forms of alienation as fewer and fewer people feel they have any control over crucial aspects of human life. (Henry, *Peripheral Capitalism and Underdevelopment in Antigua*, 115–29).

38. Matthew Quest, "Wisdom Is Plentiful Among Ordinary People to Govern: A View of Antigua's Tim Hector and Guyana's Eusi Kwayana," in *Antigua and Barbuda Review of Books*, 132.

39. See Justice Albe Sachs's "Where Are the Beautiful People?" Lecture on file with the author.

CHAPTER 4

1. Patrisse Khan-Cullors, Asha Bandele, and Angela Y. Davis. *When They Call You a Terrorist: A Black Lives Matter Memoir* (New York: St. Martin's Press, 2018), 4–5.

2. See Drucilla Cornell, *Beyond Accommodation: Ethical Feminism, Deconstruction and the Law* (New York: Routledge, 1991).

3. *Bhe and Others v. Khayelitsha Magistrate and Others* [CCT 49/03] [2004] ZACC 17.

4. Baruch Spinoza, *Ethics*, ed. G. H. R Parkinson (Oxford: Oxford University, 2000).

5. Étienne Balibar, *Spinoza and Politics* (London: Verso, 1998).

6. D. A. Masolo, "Western and African Communitarianism: A Comparison," in *African Legal Theory and Contemporary Problems*, ed. O. Onazi (Dordrecht: Martinus Nijhoff, 2004), 483–98.

7. Mabogo More, "Albert Luthuli, Steve Biko, and Nelson Mandela: The Philosophical Basis of their Thought and Practice," in *A Companion to African Philosophy* (London: Blackwell, 2005), 156–57.

8. See also, in general, Drucilla Cornell, *Law and Revolution in South Africa: uBuntu, Dignity, and the Struggle for Constitutional Transformation* (New York: Fordham University Press, 2014).

9. Carol Gilligan, *In a Different Voice: Psychological Theory and Women's Development* (London: Cambridge, 1988).

10. Simone de Beauvoir, *The Second Sex* (New York: Alfred A. Knopf, 1953).

11. John Rawls, *A Theory of Social Justice* (Cambridge: The Belknap Press, 1971) and *Political Liberalism* (New York: Columbia University Press, 1988).

12. Seyla Benhabib, *Situating the Self: Gender Community and Postmodernism in Contemporary Ethics* (New York: Routledge, 1992).

13. See Audre Lorde, *Uses of the Erotic: The Erotic as Power* (New York: Out & Out, 1978).

14. Dorothy Roberts, *Killing the Black Body: Race, Reproduction, and the Meaning of Liberty* (New York: Pantheon, 1997).

15. Lewis Gordon, *Fear of Black Consciousness* (New York: Farrar, Straus and Giroux, 2022).

16. For a longer discussion of a distinction between "liberation from" and "liberation to," see chapter 1.

17. Keeanga-Yamahtta Taylor, Barbara Smith, Beverly Smith, Demita Frazier, Alicia Garza, and Barbara Ransby, *How We Get Free: Black Feminism and the Combahee River Collective* (Chicago: Haymarket Books, 2017), 19–20.

18. Ibid., 69.

19. Drucilla Cornell and Stephen Seeley, "There's Nothing Revolutionary about a Blowjob," Social Text 32, no. 2 (Duke University Press, 2014): 1–23.

20. Taylor et al., *How We Get Free*, 127–28.

21. bell hooks, *Killing Rage: Ending Racism* (New York: Henry Holt & Company, 1996), 107.

22. Audre Lorde, *Sister Outsider: Essays and Speeches* (Trumansburg, NY: Crossing Press, 1984), 56.
23. bell hooks, *All about Love: New Visions* (New York: William Morrow, 2000).
24. Khan-Cullors et al., *When They Call You a Terrorist*, 4–5.
25. Ibid., 15.
26. Gordon, *Fear of Black Consciousness*, 132.
27. Khan-Cullors et al., *When They Call You a Terrorist*, 107.
28. Ibid., 162.
29. Ibid., 163.
30. Paget Henry, "Claudia Jones, Political Economy, and the Creolizing of Rosa Luxemburg," in *Creolizing Rosa Luxemburg*, edited by Jane Anna Gordon and Drucilla Cornell (Lanham. MD: Rowman & Littlefield, 2021), 434.
31. See also the foundational texts of creolizing: Michael Monahan's *The Creolizing Subject: Race, Reason, and the Politics of Purity* (New York: Fordham University Press, 2011) and Jane Anna Gordon's *Creolizing Fanon and Rousseau* and *Creolizing Political Theory: Reading Rousseau through Fanon* (New York: Fordham University Press, 2014).
32. Wilson Harris, *The Infinite Rehearsal* (London: Faber and Faber, 1987).
33. Cornell, *Spirit of Revolution: Beyond the Dead Ends of Man* (Cambridge: Polity, 2016) 10.
34. Gordon, *Fear of Black Consciousness*, 64–66.

CONCLUSION

1. Óscar Guardiola-Rivera, *Story of a Death Foretold: The Coup Against Salvador Allende, September 11, 1973* (New York: Bloomsbury Press, 2013), 292–93.
2. Ibid., 294.
3. Ibid.

INDEX

aesthetic ideas, 64, 87
Africa, xiii, ix, 13, 46, 47, 77, 106
African Americans, ix, xx, 39, 82; mothers, 82; women, 91–2
African National Congress (ANC), xiii, xiv, 19, 21–2, 88, 106
African philosophy, xi, 21, 67–8, 74, 85–9, 102–3
Afro-Caribbean philosophy, 102; *see also* Paget Henry
Akan, the, 101
Algerian War, 5, 7
Allende, Salvador Guillermo, 105–8
anarchy, 49
Anderson, Kevin, 114 n8
Anglo-Analytical philosophy, 9
Animal laborans, 4, 9
anti-black racism, xvi, xxi, 13, 43, 89, 92, 95, 100–101
Antigua, 70, 75–6, 96, 105
Antigua Caribbean Liberation Movement (ACLM), 76–8
apartheid, xiii–xiv, 21, 27, 68, 88, 92
Arendt, Hannah, ix, 4–11, 13–14, 19, 23, 111 n11–16, 112 n21, 112 n23, 112 n25

Asian Americans, ix
Athenian democracy, 73
authoritarianism, viii, 25
authority, 4, legal, 73; moral, 74; of men over women, 84; of sovereign, 2; phallic, 22; state's, 3, 35
Avakian, Bob, 78

Bader, Jenny Lyn, ix
Badiou, Alain, 25–6, 113 n2
Baku, 32
Bales, Kevin, 112 n17
Balibar, Étienne, 3, 6, 14, 19–20, 30, 111 n4, 112 n17, 111 n19, 111 n38–40, 113 n40–41, 113 n52, 114 n16, 118 n5
Bandele, Asha, 81 n81, 118 n1
barbarism, 58 107, 116 n14
Bay of Pigs, 106
Beauvoir, Simone de, 89
Being, 59–65, 67–8, 86
Benhabib, Seyla, 91, 118 n12
Bergson, Henri, 28, 114 n9
Berkowitz, Roger, v, ix
Bernsteinists, 50

Bhandar, Brenna, 2, 111 n6
Biden, Vice President Joe, xv
Biehl, Joao, 112 n18
Biko, Steve Bantu, 27, 118 n7
biology, 28
Bird, VC, 75, 117 n32
Birmingham (Alabama), 12
Black consciousness, xvii, 100
Black feminism thought, 95–6, 102
Black labor, 88
#BlackLivesMatter, 100
Black Lives Matter, xiii, xv–xvi, 1, 44–5, 81–2, 100, 110 n2
Black Panther Party, 13, 17–18, 20, 96; Free Breakfast for Children Program, 18
Black Power, 13, 37, 39–44, 46, 75, 97
Black radicalism, 36
"Blood Sunday," 31
Bolsheviks, 28, 35, 49, 56, 58–9, 64
Boston, xxi, 110 n13
bourgeoisie, 34, 53,
Brown, Michael, 1
Brown, Wendy, 25, 113 n1
Brown v. Board of Education, xx, 110 n12
Buchannan, Larry, Quoctrung Bui, and Jugai K. Patel, 110 n2
Budd, Billy, 8
Buenos Aires, 1
Build Back Better Bill, xvi
Bulger, Whitey, xxi

California state prisons, 11
capitalism, xviii, 33, 47–50; neoliberal, xiii–xiv, xvi; racialized, xix, xxi, 2, 10–11, 13, 15, 20, 22–3, 27, 30, 42, 44–5
Caribbean, the, xi, xix, 72, 77, 96, 102, 105; creole tradition in, 101

Caribbean Liberation Movement (ACLM), 76–8
Caribbean New Left, the, 69–72, 78
Caribbean Philosophical Association (CPA), iii, x, xii, 83
Carmichael, Stokley/Kwame Ture, 42–3, 97
Castro, Fidel, 106
Central Park, 108
Césaire, Aimé, 9, 112 n30
Charlotte Amalie, 1
Chile, 105, 107–8
Chinese Cultural Revolution, 26
citizenship, 23, 113 n41
civility, 14–15, 19–20, 23, 111 n4, 112 n17, 112 n31
Civil Rights Movement, xix, 16–17, 37–9, 42, 44, 46
civilization, 78, 81, 83
class, xiv, xviii–xix, 24–5, 9, 34–43, 68, 50–53, 58, 76, 78, 88, 95; struggle, 3
Code of Conduct, 19, 21–2
colonialism, 5–11, 13–20, 22–3, 27, 30, 42, 44–5, 62; British, 73; neo-76
colonized, the, 6–9, 13, 15, 26, 70, 75
colonizers, 8–9, 13, 101
colonization, 3, 6–7, 9, 36, 70, 73, 101–102; Portuguese, 69
Comaroff, Jean and John, 47, 115 n1
Combahee River Collective, 95–6
commodities, 92
communism, 51–2, 54, 57–8, 78, 116 n11
Communist(s), ix, 47, 106
Communist parties, 46, 48
Connor, Bull, 12
consciousness, 61, 88; racial, 42; self-, 34; *see also* Black consciousness

Index

conservatism, 85–6
Corbyn, Jeremy, 47
Cornell, Drucilla, 109 n5, 110 n11, 113 n49–51, 114 n15, 115, n41, 117 n23, 117 n30, 118 n2, 118 n8, 118, n19, 119 n30, 119 n33, 131
COVID-19, 13, 106
creolization, 14, 56, 64, 101–3
cruelty, 6, 10, 11, 13, 15, 17–20, 22–3, 27, 35, 45, 113 n41
Cuba, 25, 105–6
Cuban Missile Crisis, 106
culture, 75, 101

damned, the, 8–9, 13
Davis, Angela Y., 1–3, 10–11, 36, 112 n33–6, 118 n1
Dean, Jodi, 48, 115 n2
death, 6–10, 14
decolonial anti-violence, 8–9
decolonizing political theory, x
dehumanization, xvii, 26, 100
"de-individualization," 70
democracy/democracies, xiv–xv, 32, 45, 49, 51–5, 58, 73, 88, 106–9; bourgeoise, 50, 53, 55; participatory, 64–5, 72, 77; social, xiv–xv, 32, 88, 96
Democratic Party (US), xiv–xv
demonizing, xvii, xxii, 20, 109 n2
dialectical materialism, 37, 47–9, 59, 61, 64–5, 98–103
dialectics, 30, 36–7, 40, 47–103, 115 n39, 116 n9, 116 n14
Dialectics of Liberation Congress (1967), 40
dictatorships, 28, 51, 58, 65, 106
dignity, 28, 45, 86, 93–4, 100, 103
disempowerment, xvii, 7, 100, 117 n37
Disner, Madeleine, xi
Dorlin, Elsa, 111 n7

dreams, 11, 98
Du Bois, W.E.B., 115 n43
Dunayevskaya, Raya, xi
Dworkin, Ronald, 131

Eastwood, Clint, ix
economics, 56, 77
economic institutions, 96, 105
education, xviii, xxi, 10, 17, 34, 96
enemy (construction of), xvii–xviii, 15, 109 n7
England, 42
enslavement / slavery, 45, 51, 92
epistemic capabilities, 63
epistemic humility, 68
epistemology, 85–8
essence, 59, 68–9
ethics, 21, 67, 89–91
Eurocentrism, x–xi, 102–3
Europe, 24, 28, 57, 89, 111 n4
European philosophy, 67, 83, 85, 87, 102
evil, 8
experience, 29, 34, 37, 46, 60, 66, 100, 102–3

failure, 28, 32, 35, 42, 44, 47, 69, 94, 105–6
Fanon, Frantz, ix, xiv, 4; Arendt on, 4–11, 26–7, 36, 44, 64, 66, 89, 109n4, 112, n18, 112 n20, 109n22, 109 n23, 109 n29, 109 n31, 109 n36, 113 n42, 113 n48, 113 n53, 114 n5–6, 119 n31; on counterviolence, 11–24
fascism, xvii–xviii, 108
favelas, 6
feminism, 82–3, 89–93, 95–6, 103
flourishing, 68, 93
Floyd, George, xvi, 1–2, 44
Foucault, Michel, 3, 102, 111 n10
France, 25

freedom, xvii, xviii, 4–5, 11, 18–19, 22, 28–30, 43, 45–6, 51–4, 68–9, 72, 82, 87, 94; democratic, 107; existential, 89; reproductive, 92
Freedom Charter of the ANC, xiv, 68
Freedom Riders, 16
FRELIMO (the revolutionary party of Mozambique), 69

Gandhi, Mahatma, 3, 38
Gay Liberation Movement, 43
gender, 84, 89, 95–96, 103
genocide, 6, 22
Gilligan, Carol, 89–91, 119 n9
globalization, 117 n37
Global South, 47, 49, 66
Goddesses and Gods, 98, 106
Gold Coast, 39
Gordon, Jane Anna, v, ix–x, 115 n41, 119 n30–31, 131
Gordon, Lewis R., v, x, xx, 7, 89, 95, 99–100, 103, 109 n6, 112 n20, 112 n22, 112 n24, 113 n3, 114 n6–7, 118 n15, 119 n26; on "I can't breathe," xvi–xvii; on hypervisibility, 97; on liberation, 26–7, 96; on political responsibility, 103; on racism, 100; on violence, 7; *see also* Black consciousness
government, xiii, xviii, 8–9, 12, 19, 25, 27, 32, 45, 52, 70–73, 76, 82, 87, 96; Cuban, 106–7
governmentality, 87
Greece, 47
Guardiola-Rivera, Oscar, 107
Guevara, Che, 106
guilt, xix–xx, 99

Haiti, 25
Haitian Revolution, 45
Hani, Chris, 36

Harris, Wilson, 101–3, 119 n32
Havana, 106
health, xviii; care, 17, 96, 106
Hector, Tim, 105, 117 n33
Hegel, G.W.F., ix, 43, 50–51, 55, 57–69, 71, 74, 77–8, 111 n4, 114 n13, 116 n20; on Absolute Knowledge, 62, 65–6; on Spirit, 65–6
hegemony, 14, 19, 28, 60, 111 n6
Henry, Paget, v, x, xiii, 62–4, 65–7, 71–81, 97, 109 n3, 115 n4, 116 n20, 117 n23, 117 n32–7, 119 n30; on self-transformations," 66–70; on the ACLM, 76–7; on the creole tradition, 101–2; on the "vertical Revolution," x, xv, 67–71, 77–8, 81, 97; Three Reconstructions of Black struggles, 44–5
Henry, Paget, Jane Anna Gordon, Lewis R. Gordon, Aaron Kamugisha, and Neil Robert, 51 n15, 94 n17
Hinduism, 101
history, 3, 20, 26, 29, 36, 45–6, 51, 53–4, 57, 62–3, 66, 68, 73–4, 88; of African philosophy, 89; of white supremacy in the United States, 97
Hobbes, Thomas, 2, 87, 111 n4
Hobbesianism, 87
Homo faber, 4
hooks, bell, 96–8, 103, 119 n21, 119 n22
hope, xv, 11, 43, 98
horror, xx, 10, 27
Hudis, Peter, v, xi, 112 n18, 114 n8
humanism, 89
Hungarian Revolution, 39
Hungary, 43, 70

"I can't breathe," xvi–xvii, 1
identity, ix, 102; "politics," 43
Ignatiev, Noel, 110 n14
imagination, 10, 29–30, 33, 36, 46, 66, 114 n11
individual (the), 48, 55, 64, 67–8, 86, 87, 89, 93; trans, 67–8, 86
individualism, 67, 82, 93
Internationals, 65
invisibilization, 27
Irish American(s), xxi
Islam, 82, 101

James, C. L. R., xi, xiv, xvii, 28, 36–46, 48–9, 53–78, 95, 105, 115 n27–39, 115 n44, 116 n8–10, 116 n12–22, 117 n24, 117 n27
January 1905 general strike, 34
January 6, 2021, insurrection/attempted coup, xviii, 32
Johnson-Forest Tendency, the, xi
justice, xvii, 8, 15, 18, 22–3, 28, 69, 79, 89–94, 103, 108; social, 3
justification, 24, 62–3, 85–6, 79

Kabwe, 21
Kant, Immanuel, 29, 64–5, 87, 90–91
Karenga, Maulana (Ron), 74
Kendi, Ibram X., xvi, xix, xxi, 110 n10
Kennedy, President John F., 106
Khan-Cullors, Patrisse, 81, 98–100, 102–3, 118 n1, 119 n24–5, 119 n27
Khayamandi Township, 83–5
King, Jr., Martin Luther, 3, 16, 37–8, 113 n43
Kingdom of Ends, 87; *see also* Kant
Klansmen, 16
Kohlberg, Lawrence, 91
Knowing, 65
Kwayana, Eusi, 78

labor, 4, 9, 59–60, 67, 71–2, 78, 88, 95, 112 n26; cheap, 96; laws, 73; movement, 40, 63
Lacanian psychoanalysis, 48, 58
Lardner, Michael, x
Latin Americans, xix, 47
laws, xx, 28; labor, 73; scientific, 29, 64
leftism, 25–7, 41, 43, 48, 69–72, 78–9
legitimacy, 13, 100
Lenin, Vladimir, xiv, 28, 35–6, 48–61, 64–5, 68, 70–71, 116 n3–5, 116 n14n
Leninism, 55, 61, 70–71
Lesbian and Gay Sangoma Association, 84
Libya, 77
Locke, John, 2, 111 n5
London (UK), 40
Lorde, Audre, 91, 97, 102–3, 118 n13, 119 n22
Los Angeles, xix
love, 97–8, 102–3
Luxemburg, Rosa, x–xi, xiv–xv, 28–39, 42, 44–6, 49–50, 58–60, 63, 65–6, 102, 107, 114 n8, 114 n10, 114 n19, 114 n21
lynching, 2, 15, 17, 44–5

MacDonald, Michael, xxi, 110 n13
MacGrogan, Maureen, x
MAGA, 13
Mamdani, Mahmood, 111 n8
Mandela, President Nelson, xiii, 3, 118 n7
Mao Zedong, 78
Maoism, 82
Marcuse, Herbert, 29, 114 n13
marketing, xviii, 76
marketplace, xviii, 85
Marx, Karl, 7

Marxism, x, 36, 39–41, 48, 57, 71, 91, 95, 98
Marxist Education Project, x
Masolo, D. A., 86, 118 n6
Massachusetts Racial Imbalance Act, 110 n15
May 1968, 26
Mbembe, Achille, 112 n18
melancholia, 25
metaphysics, 38, 81, 101–2
Monahan, Michael J., ix, 116 n20, 119 n31
monsters, xvi, 7
Montgomery Bus Boycott, 37–8, 43
morality, 3, 12, 20, 73, 86–7, 89–91, 103
More, Mabogo P., 86, 89, 118 n7
Morrison, Toni, xvii–xviii, 109 n7, 113 n45–6
Moscow, 31
Mozambican liberation, 69

NAACP (National Association for the Advancement of Colored People), 37
Nariva, Oropouche, and Caroni swamps, 73
National Guard, the, xx
nationalization, xiv
National Research Foundation Chair (South Africa), xi–xii
Nazi Germany, 4
Négritude, 43
"negroes," 37, 39–45
New Beginning Movement (NBM), 72–5, 77–8
New Left, 41, 43, 70–72, 78
Newton, Huey P., 18, 113 n45
Newtonian mechanics, 29
New York City, 11, 41, 83
Ngcobo, Justice, 84
Nite, 74, 117 n29, 117 n31

Nkrumah, Kwame, 36, 42, 115 n36
novel coronavirus SARS-CoV-2, 1
Nyerere, Julius, 74

Oakland (California), 33
Obama, President Barack, xv
Occupy (movement), 47
Oil Field Workers Trade Union, 71–2
ontology, 13–14, 50–51, 64, 85–6, 89; Lacanian, 58; of revolution, 2t6
oppression, xvii, 40–42, 45, 55, 62, 72, 82, 94–6, 106
Orisha Spirituality, xix, xx

Paris, Commune, the, 26, 51, 56, 58
Parks, Rosa, 37
Parliamentary representation, 75–6, 96
party, the, 25, 27–8, 33–40, 43, 47–62, 64–73, 75, 77
patriarchy, 83, 95–7
Patterson, Orlando, 30, 114 n14
personhood, 2, 68
pessimism, 88
phenomenological suspension, 63
philosophy, 38, 62, 67–8, 74, 83, 85–9, 102–3, 111 n4, 131; Anglo-analytic, ix; political, 23. *See also* African philosophy, European philosophy
Pinochet Ugarte, President General Augusto José Ramón, 107–8
Podemos, 47
police, the, xv–xvi, 1–3, 9, 12–13, 15–16, 19, 22, 37, 44–5, 72–3, 110 n1
political, the, 35
political action, 5, 9, 11, 13, 15–17, 20–23, 26–7, 31, 33–4, 41–56,
political reality, xvii, 23

political spirituality, 11, 47, 49, 59, 66–8, 77–9, 102–3
political theory, x, 3–6, 11, 16, 38, 60, 88
politics, ix, 5, 11, 26–7, 36, 43, 48, 56–7, 75, 77, 113 n41;
liberal conception of, 2, 11; of anti-violence, 14; party, 72; revolutionary, 49–50; socialist, 95; US electoral, xiv
populism, xvii–xviii
poverty, xiv, 6
power, xiv, xvii–xviii, xix, 4, 7–13, 19, 27, 32, 41, 48, 68, 77, 110 n9; bureaucratic, 72; collective, 9; creative, 30, 39, 44; imperial, 6; People's, 75–8; state, xiii, xvi, 31, 35, 49, 105, 107; transfer of, 51; *see also* Black Power
privatization, xviii
progress, xv
progressive, xv, 97
proletariat, the, 31, 33–5, 39–40, 43, 51, 53–4, 57, 65, 70–72, 106–7
property, xiii, 1–3, 15–16, 19, 23, 29, 42, 76
psychoanalysis, 48, 59

Quest, Matthew, 72–3, 78, 117 n27

race, xix, 88, 92, 95
racism, x, xvi–xxi, 1–2, 8, 10, 13, 36, 91–8, 100–101, 110 n7; anti-, 44, 89, 92, 88, 95. *See also* antiblack racism
rape, 6, 9, 22
rationality, 4, 22, 90
Rawls, John, 91, 118 n11
reason, xvi, 27, 29, 64, 68, 83, 90, 102
Reconstruction and Development Programme (RDP), xiii

revolution(s), x, xiii–xvii, xix, 4–5, 11–15, 19, 23, 25–46, 50–51, 53–60, 62–71, 78–9, 81–2, 95, 97, 100, 105–8, 116 n14; Chinese Cultural, 26; Russian, 26, 33, 37, 49– 50, 55–6, 65
revolutionaries, 17, 39, 59, 63, 65, 69, 82
Revolutionary Afghan Women's Association (RAWA), 18, 82
Riga, 32
rights, xviii, 40, 82, 94
rioters, xviii
riots, 42
Roberts, Alfie, 70–71
Roberts, Dorothy, 118 n14
Russia, 25–6, 31–7, 48–50, 52–6, 58, 60, 65
Russian Empire, 31
Russian Social Democratic Labour Party (RSDLP), 49
Russo-Japanese War, 31
Rutgers University, 131

Sachs, Justice Albie, 19, 21, 79, 117 n19
Sanders, Senator Bernie, xiv–xv, 47, 106
Sangoma, 84
Sartre, Jean-Paul, 6–7, 43, 115 n40
science, 59, 64–5, 68, 98
Seeley, Stephen, xi, 102, 118 n19
self-defense, 3, 14, 17–18, 22–3, 96, 111 n7
sexism, 47, 96
sexual difference, 90, 94
Shack Dwellers Movement, 88
Sharpeville, 41
Simondon, Gilbert, 67
Smith, Barbara, 95, 118 n17
social contract, 2, 87

social institutions, xv, 17–18, 66, 69, 75, 78
socialism, xiii, xvi, 11, 27–33, 36–7, 40–45, 47, 51–60, 64, 66, 68–75, 78, 8, 83, 88, 96–7, 105, 107, 116 n14; democratic, 32–3, 75, 81, 83, 88, 96, 105, 107–8. 117 n32
Socialist Workers Party Convention in 1948, 39, 55, 62
solidarity, 33, 68, 88
South Africa, x, xi–xii, xiii–xiv, 19, 21–2, 25, 27, 67–8, 83–94, 106, 131
South African Constitutional Court, 84
South African Defense Forces, 22
South America, 77, 106–7
sovereignty, 2
Soviet Union, 51, 55, 60, 77, 106–7
Spain, 47
speech, 8, 42
Spinoza, Benedict, 67, 85, 114 n15, 118 n4
St. Petersburg, 31–3, 37, 41
Stalin, Joseph, 65, 78
Stalinism, 47
struggle, xiii–xiv, xvi, xvii, xix, xxi, 3, 7–8, 11, 14, 17–23, 26–46; armed, xiii, xvi, 3, 7, 11, 14, 18–19, 21–8, 105, 107; Black, 37, 40–46, 61; class, 34–5, 72; endless, xvi
Syriza, 47

Tambo, Oliver, 2
Tanzania, 25
Tartar, Ellen, ix
Taylor, Keeanga-Yamahtta, 25
Tbilisi, 32
Tehran, 1
Terreblanche, Solomon, xiii–xiv, 88, 109 n1

terror, xviii, 19, 22, 25; reign of, 14; state of, 9; War on, 3
terrorism, 13, 15, 21
terrorists, 17–18, 20, 82, 99, 107
Third World, 7, 40
Tokyo, 1
toxic dumping, 6
transindividuality, 67–8, 85
Trinidad, 70, 72–3, 96, 105
Trotsky, Leon, 55–6, 63, 65–6
Trotskyism, 28, 37, 55, 57, 62–3
Trump, President Donald, xv, 13, 20
truth, 50, 58, 64–5, 98, 103, 116 n14
Tyson, Neil deGrasse, 81

uBuntu/Ubuntu, x–xi, 21, 67–8, 74, 83–9, 92–4, 102, 111 n4, 111 n50, 117 n29, 118 n8, 131
uBuntu Project, x–xi, 83–4, 89, 131
uBuntu Women's Center, 84
Ujamaa Socialism, 74
ukase, 29
uMkhonto we Sizwe (MK; Spear of the Nation), 19
United States of America (USA), xv, xix, 1, 3, 40–3, 45, 61, 89, 91–3, 96–7, 102, 106–7, 115 n35
universality, 43, 46, 51
University of Cape Town, xii
University of Chicago, 107

violence, ix, xx, 1–23, 35, 38–9, 31–42, 44, 52, 68, 101, 107–8, 111 n4, 112 n26; counter, 9, 10, 14, 15, 16–20, 111 n 4
voice(s), xvi, 42, 58, 72, 76, 91
voting, xiii, xviii, xx, 16, 19, 82

war, 5, 18, 22, 44, 56, 82, 106
Warren, Senator Elizabeth, xv
Warsaw, 32
Watts, xix–xx

Waverly Diner, xi
Weber, Max, 2, 111 n4
whiteness, xix, xxii
work, xx–xxi, 4, 9, 21, 32, 34, 51–3, 61, 71, 95; -day, 35
workers, xi, 31–5, 51–2, 54–71, 76, 77, 95, 105, 107, 108; see also *proletariat*

Wynter, Sylvia, 43, 64, 116 n11

X, Malcom, 17, 113 n44

Žižek, Slavoj, 48

About the Author

Drucilla Cornell is an emeritus professor of political science, women's studies, and comparative literature at Rutgers University. She is a playwright and also launched the uBuntu Project in South Africa in 2003 and has been working with the project ever since. Professor Cornell's theoretical and political writings span a tremendous range of both topics and disciplines. From her early work in critical legal studies and feminist theory to her more recent work on South Africa, transitional justice, and the jurisprudence of Ronald Dworkin, Professor Cornell continues to think through new and evolving issues in philosophy and politics of global significance. Her latest title, coauthored with Stephen Seely, is called *The Spirit of Revolution: Beyond the Dead Ends of Man*, and she recently edited *Creolizing Rosa Luxemburg* with Jane Anna Gordon.

www.ingramcontent.com/pod-product-compliance
Lightning Source LLC
Chambersburg PA
CBHW031712230426
43668CB00006B/186